THE PRESIDENT AND "FELLOWS" OF YALE.

YALE ⁂ HUMOR:

A COLLECTION OF

HUMOROUS ⁑ SELECTIONS

FROM THE

UNIVERSITY ⁑ PUBLICATIONS.

EDITED AND ARRANGED BY S. A. YORK, JR., YALE, '90.

NEW HAVEN, CONN.:

S. A. YORK, JR., 201 DURFEE HALL.

1890.

5588
.1757

Press of The Stafford Printing Co,
86 to 90 Crown Street,
New Haven, Conn.

INTRODUCTORY.

TO those into whose hands this volume will probably fall, nothing can afford a more complete interpretation of its aims than the mere mention of its title. The slightest familiarity with academic life is co-existent with a knowledge of the humorous side of an undergraduate course, and in the selection of the contents an effort has been made to conform as closely as possible to the requirements of a volume which should be recognized at once as Yale in tone by Yale men and their friends.

It is for the sake of collecting and perpetuating in convenient form, the best humorous articles treating of college customs and topics, that this collection has been published, and it is on this point it should be judged without regard to any literary merit.

The annual "Fence Orations" form such a prominent feature in Yale life that it was considered advisable to include the one which seemed the most typical. Accordingly the Sophomore oration of Mr. Isaac Bromley, Jr., '81, has been selected, this, at the time, having attracted wide attention, being re-printed in all the leading papers.

The illustrations have been taken from the *Yale Record*, and the remaining matter from the *Record* and the *Courant*, On account of the failure of the earlier editors of these papers to publish indexes, the names of a number of writers whose articles have been selected could not be ascertained, and it was thought that rather than publish a partial list, a complete omission would be preferable. In default, therefore, of any other means, this opportunity is taken of acknowledging the indebtedness to the unknown humorists, hoping that they will pardon a few unimportant alterations.

CONTENTS.

ILLUSTRATIONS.

PAGE

President and "Fellows" of Yale, The, - *Frontispiece*
Ah ! Quel Malheur, - - - - 70
Alas, Alack ! - - - - 58
All the World's a Stage, - - - 42
Atte Christmas-tyde, - - - 57
At the Game, - - - - 37
Before and After, - - - - 46
Campaign at College, The, - - 13
Chart of the Campus, A. - - - 21
Chip from an Ancient Tablet, A. - - 30
Circumstances Alter Appearances, - - 18
College Songs, - - - - 51
Composite Photography, - - - 23
Corporation's Donkey Party, The, - - 48
Dainty Little Maiden, - - - 66
Degeneration of the Sash Craze, The, - - 65
Dude that Didn't Dance, The, - - 19
Effects of a College Vacation, - - 59
Farmington Car, The, - - - 71
Founding of Yale, Ye, - - - 74
He Used It, - - - - 36
It's an Ill Wind, etc., - - - 39
"Jes a Few Mo' Lef," - - - 17
Lady or the Tiger, The, - - - 45
Mamma Harvard, - - - - 15
Modern Dress, - - - - 35
My Chum's Sister, - - - 26
My Pipe, - - - - 28
"Nigger Baby" in Ancient Rome, - - 49
On the Right Trail, - - - 53
Peeler's Mishap, The, - - - 41
Positively the Worst Yet, - - - 40
Quantitative Analysis, A, - - - 29
Scheme for Collecting for Crew Trophies, - 14
Signs of Fall, - - - - 52
Sleighing, - - - - 33
Some Tennis Expressions, - - - 50
St. Elihu's Annual Game, - - - 10

PAGE

Street Urchin, The, - - - - 27
Thou Maiden Sweet, - - - 64
Troubadour's Wooing, A, - - - 25
Unanimity, - - - - 34
Unknown, - - - - 67
Yale Tank, The, - - - - 56
Washington's Birthday, - - - 31
Why Not ? - - - - 69

PROSE.

At Last ! - - - - 48
Chaperone, The, - - - 20
Chestnut, The, - - - - 50
Child's Dream of an Ideal Father, A, - - 18
College Symphony, The, - - - 36
Conversations, - - - - 63
Extract from a Novel on Yale Life, - - 40
Fables, - - - - 68
Fearful Charge, A, - - - 58
Fence Oration, A, - - - 76
Football, - - - - 14
Founding of Yale, Ye, - - - 74
From Advance Sheets, - - - 32
Geological Metaphysics, - - - 37
George Washington, - - - 68
Gym. Ghost's Revenge, The, - - 10
Infra Dig, - - - - 70
Junior English, - - - - 24
Letter from American School at Athens, - - 56
Military Tactics, - - - - 12
New Dormitory, A, - - - 28
Old Curiosity Shop, The - - 46
One Week at Yale, - - - 16
Outrageous Charges, - - - 58
Parable, A, - - - - 72
Prom. Examination, - - - 72
"Record" Series of Text Books, The, - - 39
Reflections, - - - - 38
Rowdyism, Ruffianism, and Rusticity, - - 70

	PAGE
So To Speak,	44
Stag's Diary, A,	22
Stray "Lit." Article, A.	17
To Whom it May Concern.	33
"The Tutor, Mr. Barlow,"	26
Valuable Remnant, A,	64
Vision of Mirzah, The,	9

VERSE.

	PAGE
Ah, Quel Malheur!	70
Alas, Alack!	58
All the World's a Stage,	42
Atte Chrismas-tyde,	57
At the German	22
At the Masquerade,	38
Bell, The,	11
Blood Will Tell,	24
Constant Lover, Ye,	16
Dainty Little Maiden,	66
Dude that Didn't Dance, The,	19
Farmington Car, The,	71
Fickle Love, O,	34
Modern Dress,	35
My Chum's Sister,	26

	PAGE
My Pipe,	28
No Rose Without It's Thorn.	48
On Handshaking,	28
Peeler's Mishap, The,	41
Poor Little Rose,	44
Recitation in May,	49
Rondeau,	30
Sandwiches,	68
Senior Prom. The,	18
Sleighing,	33
Song, A,	40
Street Urchin, The,	27
Tailor, The,	32
Thou Maiden Sweet,	64
Trinity Chimes,	12
Troubadour's Wooing, A,	25
Unknown,	67
With a Box of Candy,	36

MISCELLANEOUS.

	PAGE
Glimpse of Yale Journalism, A,	54
Marking System Exposed, The,	73
Melasippos,	60

YALE · HUMOR.

THE VISION OF MIRZAH.

[REVISED EDITION.]

A ND it came to pass that on a certain evening I dined with friends, and was borne home as the Wain was in the west, sinking, and Lucifer was casting his rays obliquely down, heralding the coming of rosy morn. And it seemed that I did behold two Wains and two Lucifers, but when I told my comrades so, they did turn my remark to ridicule and laughter. And they removed my doublet and hose, and commended me to the drowsy arms of Morpheus.

And as I lay, I saw a vision, and behold, a long bridge appeared, over which multitudes were passing. And as I looked again, I saw that on entering the bridge they were but youths, callow and beardless, but as they emerged upon the other side they were older, and had hair upon their faces, and some had it shaven off, and some had let it grow, upon their lips, and their cheeks, and their chins. Then I drew nearer, for to see what this might mean.

And behold, there were many coaches approaching the bridge, and some coaches brought but one youth, and others brought many. And the youths who came with the coaches looked, some eager, some frightened, but all were callow youths, and had a broken string tied to them. And it did seem to me that the strings were very like to those which women do use to tie aprons with.

And I looked again, and behold, the youths did form themselves into a group to mount the approach to the bridge, and at the entrance thereof there was a great pitfall, exceeding difficult to pass, and some unwary youths did fall through and others stumbled and were hurt, but the greater part got safe over. And when they were started, behold certain men did meet them, to go with them on their journey as guides. And these guides did instruct them how much ground to get over in one day, and how they should get over the ground. And it did seem to me that the journey would be exceeding hard to travel without these guides.

And I saw, at the entrance to the bridge, a stable, and in that stable were many horses. And many of the travelers did purchase these beasts, since the way was hard and long, and they were not strong enough to walk. Now these horses were of divers colors and sizes, but there were two breeds which the youths did affect more than any other, and one of these was a certain Grecian breed, and the other was of Latin stock. So the youths were started on their way.

Now, when they had traveled some distance, behold, a grievous pitfall stood in their way, like unto the one at the entrance, but deeper, and harder to pass, and there was much fear and trembling among the youths, as they wondered how they should pass it. And those who were foremost did pass it without ado, but those who were hindmost had much trouble to do so. And the greater part left their steeds, and making a great run, did strive to jump it, and most did succeed, but a few fell clean through and could not get back again. And some daring fellows clung to their horses and strove to make them leap over the gulf, but this is attended with much danger, for few horses there be that can jump these pitfalls, and few youths there be who can manage them skilfully enough to make them.

And now the way was smooth again, and the youths moved on. But there were one or two who fell off the bridge, not being able to keep straight. And yet these did not fall the entire distance, but were held suspended in the air for a long time, and when they regained the bridge they were obliged to mount horses and gallop hard to overtake their mates. And these men were the ones most likely to be dropped through the pitfalls by the way.

And as the youths passed along, the pitfalls grew less wide, and easier to pass. There were eight of these

ST. ELIHU'S ANNUAL GAME OF "PIGS IN CLOVER."

by the way, but the bridge was divided into four divisions. And I heard one youth tell another that in times past there was a dragon guarding the entrance to the fourth part of the bridge, and that dragon's name was Astronomicus, and that he was very hard to pass, until his teeth were drawn by a good knight, Sir Public Opinion. Now the dragon is less formidable than before, and most men may pass him without molestation.

Now, when the youths had embarked upon the fourth part of the bridge, the way was easy. And as I looked back, behold, three other groups had started on the bridge, and each was larger than the one before it. And I looked further, and behold more coaches came, and all were laden with comely boys, who looked eagerly toward the bridge, as if longing to embark upon it.

But now the youths I had been following had neared the end, and the way became easier, and the last pitfall was very narrow and short, and all crossed it in safety. And when they came to the end of the bridge, they seemed loth to depart. And I saw many fair dames who walked with them, and I heard music and dancing. And then the youths planted a goodly vine and embraced with many tears, and departed, carrying each man a bit of parchment, with something written thereon.

Then I cast in my mind for the reason of this, and I could not tell, for there was no one whom I could ask. And I saw a man standing by the gate. He it was who had given out the bits of parchment. And I said, Learned sire, tell me, I pray, what this may mean. And he took me to the entrance and said unto me, My son, read that. And I looked, and beheld, graven in stone over the portal, a legend reading thus : " Lux et Veritas."

And I awoke, and behold, it was all a dream.

THE BELL.

After Edgar A. Poe.

I. 7 A. M.

HEAR the Chapel with it's bell,
   Booming bell,
While with the woolly blankets its noise I try to quell,
How it roars, roars, roars,
In the morning bleak and grey!
When my sleep I'm most enjoying,
Comes its howl all rest destroying,
Driving visions sweet away,
With its bang, bang, bang,
And its clang, clang, clang,   [swell,
With its fiendish clash and clatter on the ever louder
     O! that bell, bell, bell, bell,
     Bell, bell, bell !
O! the sounding and the pounding of that bell !

II. 10 P. M.

Hear the Chapel with its bell,
   Jolly bell,
What a shout of victory does its joyful notes now tell !
Through the summer's evening light,
Far into the happy night,
Comes its merry, ringing note,
     Sounding out
" Yale, old Yale's the winning boat !"
Saying over, over, over in a never ceasing rote,
     This one shout,
And its story gladly tells,
While the mucker with the crackers loudly yells.
     And the fire,
     Burning higher,
Eli's triumph brightly swells,
Nothing ever, ever, quells   [louder
Either loud exploding powder or the cheering ever
The glad and joyful ringing of the bell—
     Of the bell, bell, bell, bell,
     Bell, bell, bell—
The clanging and the whanging of the bell.

THE GYM. GHOST'S REVENGE.

AS I was walking down Chapel street the other day,
I saw the Boom for a new Gym. picking his way
carefully across the street and rolling up the bottom of
his trousers to keep them from the mud and slush. I
never had a good look at this Boom before, though I had
seen him in print numberless times ; and struck by his
excessive paleness and emaciation, I was impelled to
ask him the cause for it. Wrapping a copy of the
News several times around his attenuated shoulders,
he told me the following story:

"I was returning from a small party of Yale grad-
uates one night where I had been exerting my influence, and to calm myself before retiring, I leisurely
strolled through the campus towards the gym. I do
not known what possessed me to try the door, but
finding it unlocked to my surprise, I entered. All was
pitch dark inside, and I groped my way to the inside
door. A shudder ran through me as the outer door
closed with a bang that was dismally re-echoed several
times throughout the large room, especially as I fancied
I heard the rowing-weights in motion, then somebody
jumping on the springboard, the clink of the dumb-
bell, and an occasional thump of Indian clubs. The
creaking of the wrist machine and rattle of the parallel
bars were too distinct to be mistaken. I was chained
to the spot and not able to budge from fright as I de-
tected in the gloomy distance, with a fearful gaze, a
tall thin form approaching. It seized the horizontal
bar and commenced to perform various gyrations on it.
By the aid of a single beam that for an instant came
through the window and fell obliquely across the floor,
I could discern a ghastly bloodless face, long bony
arms, a ribbed chest, and fleshless legs. Suddenly the
figure seemed to be aware of my presence, for with a
hollow rattle of its teeth it vaulted toward me. I was
transfixed with horror. The cold perspiration stood in
drops on my body. It pointed at me a long bony
finger. I sank to the floor. . . . . .
When I recovered consciousness I found the figure
standing near me. Noticing my improved condition,
it beckoned me to follow while the wild gleam in its
bloodshot eyes indicated the uselessness of resistance.
It led me, first, to the chest weights, and seizing one
pair itself, signed to me to do likewise. We pulled
until my arms became utterly limp, when it ceased, and
leading me to the other end of the room, seized a pair
of dumb-bells, handing me a 16 lb. pair. Here again
the misery was prolonged, until I became faint from
over-exertion. After using the parallel bars and other
apparatus in like manner, it then led the way down
stairs to the hydraulic rowing-weights and placing itself
in the stroke's seat, assigned me the next seat behind,
and indicating to me to follow, started off with a forty-
four stroke. I mechanically obeyed. On, on we rowed,
the ghostly apparition seeming never to tire. Already
my arms were almost helpless, my back tired out and
every muscle on the point of completely giving way.
"Shade of Cooper," I mentally exclaimed, "how long
is this agony to last!" At this moment the stroke
went up to forty-six. I slid to and fro in the seat like
a pendulum, rapidly losing all consciousness. My head
drooped to one side, my arms were benumbed, my
whole body as if paralyzed. How long we kept this
up I can't tell, but I was suddenly brought back to
consciousness by my tormentor, who, grasping my arm,
assisted me up-stairs to the outside doors, where with
a hissing 'that's what you get for wanting to remove
me !' it left me. Somewhat revived by the fresh air,
I staggered down the street to the corner, where I fell
and was picked up and cared for by some editors returning from their annual supper."

"Do you expect to recover?" I ventured.

"Well, I'm getting stouter and stronger, and I expect——" but at this moment a gust of wind carried him a half a block down the street, and the rest of his answer was lost.

MILITARY TACTICS.

(As taught in the Cleveland and Hendricks Army of Yale College.)

SCENE—Front of Durfee. Time, 6.45 P. M. One Colonel, two Captains, three Lieutenants, a drum corps of twelve and sixteen privates appear on the scene.

First officer—Company A, fall in! Say, get in fellows. No, you want to face to the right. There, that's good. Now look out for the next command. When I say "left face," you all must turn around to your left. See? Now! Left FACE! O, turn quickly! Perhaps you expect to wait there until an earthquake shakes you around! Company, count FOURS! Now remember your numbers! At the command 'Fours right,' each four comes around to the right. Now! Fours right! What are you waiting for in that rear four? Hang it, I didn't say *fives* right. Get back to your place in line. Now move right on. Don't halt! What in thunder are you halting for? Can't I make a suggestion without having you all clustering around my knees to hear it? Now! Keep step with the drum. The drummers can't, but perhaps you can. Now look out! Company HALT! That means *stop!* Forward MARCH! Hold on, you are running into that company! Stop! Say, what are you doing! Guide *left!* Mark time, MARCH! Don't stop! Hang it, I didn't say halt. Now we're all right. Go ahead. Hurry up, why don't you? That other company is way ahead. Oh, I beg your pardon, I didn't give any order! Forward MARCH! Keep close together. Look out for your step. Be very careful about this next order! Company on the left, front into line to the left, double-quick time, MARCH! Run! come up and get in here! That back four come back from that side of the street; you belong on the other end of this line. Guide *right!* You've got a dandy line; now keep it. Look out for this wheel. Close in quick, we're coming to it. Company right wheel—stop wheeling till I say 'March.' Get back there on the left. MARCH! Come out there in the middle. Oh, heavens! what a wheel! I didn't mean a cog-wheel! Hold on there, you pivot! What are you coming over here for? You ought to stay right in your place. Well, get back into place everybody, and see if there is any way in which you can walk to the next corner without running out of the street. Don't you see these people can't understand such complicated evolutions? They never saw a prize drill. I know it's hard work for you to refrain from giving an exhibition of all marching movements while you are going half a block, but you must restrain yourselves. Company left forward, right shoulder ARMS! Fours left, and get around that corner. *No!* No! I mean, MARCH! Company HALT! Right DRESS! Well, why don't you right dress? Be kind enough to move back a little in the middle. Yes, I said *back in the middle.* Thunderation! *Get back in the middle.* Excuse me for interrupting you there in the middle, but when you get through looking at those girls on the left, just dress a little to the right. FRONT! I see you are all looking to the front already, but never mind. I like to go through the forms just for fun. Right FACE! Turn around to the right. Come back again. I forgot I had something to say to you. Gentlemen, you drill finely! Our company is the best in the battalion. We are invited to Lake Saltonstall for a parade, and hope to make an excursion to Savin Rock before long. The glorious National Democratic Committee will pay for our whole uniform and $4 apiece besides. As this money is not to be paid to us until the 5th of November, we will have to advance it now. Let me again congratulate you on your glorious cause, your fine appearance and excellent drilling. Company break ranks, MARCH!

TRINITY CHIMES.

HOW sweet, when twilight falls,
  The bell whose music hallows—
The rustic peal that calls
  Along the dewy fallows.
In notes subdued and clear,
And fading on the ear,
Leaves on the chastened sense
Its mellow evidence.
*   *   *   *   *   *   *

Ye Gods! what fiendish noise
  That rips the evening air,
Upsets my equipose
  And drives me from my chair!
  I hear a sound of war
From highest belfry pealing,
  As of discordant nations;
    A discord, jangling sore,
An inward strife revealing
  Of stiff denominations.

I hear a hideous din
  That scares the paling moon,
  That strives to be a tune
And knocks my windows in.
Oh, Mr. Edgar Poe,
  The bells once more to harp on
  Your fluent quill pray sharpen,
The bells need sharping so.

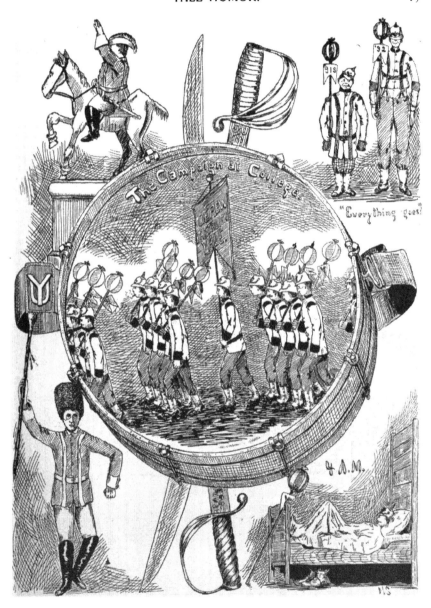

FOOT-BALL.

ILIUM *vs.* ARGOS.

SAFFRON-MANTLED morn was painting the eastern sky red, when the horse-training Trojans and the bronze-clad Greeks came together on the Ilian plain for their game of foot-ball.

Then they cast lots for referee, and every man wrote the name of Nestor on his tablet and cast it into the urn; thus Nestor, the rose-geranium knight, was chosen. Then goddess-born Achilles, dear to Mars, standing up, harangued and spoke a behest :

"Hear me, ye horse-wearying Trojans and azure-capped Greeks, that I may tell you what my soul in my breast commands me. Let us now decide by lot who may have the kick-off, ye or me, for thus is the will of wide-ruling Zeus."

Verily he thus having spoken thereupon sat down, and all murmured assent with their lips. Then Agamemnon, brave son of Atreus, and Hector, descendant of Laomedon, cast lots into the helmet. And Geranium Nestor shook the helmet, and a lot leapt forth. And the clear-voiced herald bore it through the throng, nor did Hector recognize it, but when he came to Agamemnon, the far-ruling son of Atreus, he, taking it, cast it down upon the ground, and haranguing spoke winged words :

"My friends, the lot is mine ; and I at least rejoice in heart, for I think we can weary the Trojans."

Thus he spoke, but Hector, replying, said :

"Truly, O Atreides, the sight of thee is sufficient to weary even him who is bravest." So saying, he placed his men in line, and the rank-breaking Achilles, son of Peleus, good at the war-cry, took the ball in his hand and dribbled it to Ajax Oïleus, but he took it under his arm and hastened, rejoicing in his speed, to run through the Trojan line, but Apollo tripped him, and he fell, exclaiming, "Down !"

Then, O Ajax, the end of life would have appeared to thee at the hands of the Trojans, had not Diomed, son of Tydeus, running up, warded off black fate ; and Achilles, taking the ball, snapped it back to Teucer, and he threw it to Agamemnon, saying :

"Now, far-ruling Atreides, be a man, and remember the ancient valor of thy forefathers."

Thus he spoke, nor did the son of Atreus disobey, but passed the ball to Ajax Telamon, the bulwark of the Greeks, and he forced it through the Trojan phalanx, and placed it upon the teeming earth, as when the freshman, having escaped the sophomores in the rush, breaking through their line, gains the road and goes on his way, rejoicing in his might. Thus did Ajax, of the seven-fold canvas jacket, make a touchdown. Then Teucer held the ball, and Ulysses, son of Laertes, struck it with his foot, and far on high it went through the goal posts and the flaming ether, as when a bird, glorying in his new-found wings, leaveth his perch on the fence, and cleaveth the flaming ether,

NOTHING MERCENARY ABOUT THIS.

Scheme suggested for collecting money for Crew Trophies.

Mamma Harvard : "No, Johnny, you can't go to the Polo Grounds and play with Eli, you may only play in his back-yard or in yours."

nor doth he stop until Huyler's is reached. Thus flew the ball struck by Ulysses, and crest-waving Hector, skilled with the ashen spear, received it as it fell, and cloud-compelling Zeus thundered fearfully from Ida, and the referee called time. Then Hector, standing forth, harangued and spoke winged words:

"Hear me, ye Zeus-nurtured Trojans and canvas-clad Greeks, that I may tell you what my soul in my breast commands me :

"Let us now cease from man-ennobling foot-ball for to-day ; night is approaching, and it is best to obey night, but afterwards we will again play, until some god shall separate us, and give victory to one or the other."

Thus he spoke, and all the Achæans shouted assent with their lips. And all night long they feasted, the Greeks and the Trojans, and they set up many cases, and some pawned their watches, and some their hats, and some their coats, nor did any one lack an equal share of the banquet. But Agamemnon and Achilles strove in fierce conflict about the gate-money, who should have the greater share. Then Achilles was wroth, and said that he would play no more, and that Agamemnon and the eleven could be hanged.

But the night was ended, and rosy-fingered morn kissed the lips of the Greeks and awoke them, and they took breakfast throughout their eating clubs and training tables.

Then Hector, wise in counsel, made a touch-down, but did not kick a goal, for Athene turned the ball aside. Then Ajax dribbled the ball to Patroclus, and he, seizing it, went towards Troy. But Hector tackled him, and he fell, as when the low-stand freshman, loaded with conditions, falls from his class, and is swallowed up by Hopkins. So fell the mighty Patroclus, counsellor of touch-downs, and his limbs relaxed, and his soul went down into Hades. But the ire of Achilles was kindled, and, putting away his wrath against Agamemnon, he once more entered the conflict. And he tackled Hector, and threw him upon the earth, so that his soul went down to the house of Hades, who put him on ice. Then Paris disabled Achilles, slayer of Hector, and mighty wrath seized the Greeks, that they rushed the Trojans, as when the sophomores, in line, against the freshmen rush, and the dogs do eat of the fragments ; and not one of the Trojans escaped save Æneas, who sailed away in a sea-traversing ship and came to New Jersey, and the muddy shores, and placed his mantle upon the shoulders of the Jersey men, skilled to kick. But the Greeks brought their tunics to New England, to the College of Elms, wherefore I boast that their sons will ever be valiant in the game.

YE CONSTANT LOVER.

I CANNOTT leave ye olde love:
Ye new love will nott yielde,
And 'tis nott welte, forsooth, to dwelle
Alone on Life's broad Fielde.

Sweete May is faire as Roses
That round ye Trellis twine,
And Anne is fairer far than she:—
But—zounds!—she won't be mine.

I kiss my May twice weeklie,
And whysper " I am true,"
I pleade wyth Anne ye other nights:—
Alas, I vainlie sue!

I'll aske sweete Anne to wed me;
And, if she says me nay,
I'll greve no more; but leve ye Doore
And go to faythfull May.

I cannott leve ye olde Love:
Ye new Love will nott yielde,
And 'tis not welle, forsooth, to dwelle
Alone on Life's broad Fielde.

ONE WEEK AT YALE.

ONCE there was a good little boy in Gotham who read the *Sun* and *Herald*, every word, and believed it all. His father was bald and wore spectacles, and he read the papers and believed it all. But his Uncle Jim was a wicked scoffer. He laughed and said he had been to Yale and he guessed he knew. So when the right time came and the good little Algernon had read four books of Cæsar, and seven orations of Cicero, and twenty-five hundred lines of Ovid's Metamorphoses, and the two books of Euclid, and the Virgil, and Homer, and all that, Uncle Jim's counsel prevailed, and with many tears and embraces and last injunctions, his father and mother took leave of little Algernon. But Uncle Jim, the wicked scoffer, only laughed.

The good little Algernoon was most expressly enjoined not to go out after dark and never to sit in his room without a full suit of bullet-proof armor, "for,'' as his sage parent observed, "it is a well-known fact that the whole college is engaged in a drunken riot every night, and bullets are continually flying across the campus."

On the way up from New York there were three collisions. Little Algernon's bullet-proof armor saved his life, and as everyone else got off and walked whenever they came to a dangerous place—which was all the way—no one was hurt.

Algernon skipped up back streets to the lodging carefully selected by his thoughtful parents. That it might be comparatively safe, the room was as far as possible from the campus. Our hero trembled himself to sleep and woke at five o'clock next morning, surprised to find himself alive and whole, and neither burned at the stake, nor drowned, nor buried alive, nor dangled from the face of East Rock by wicked sophs.

He wrote a letter to his father, one to his mother, one to his little sister Julia, cut off one or two doubtful buttons and sewed them on firm, ate a hasty breakfast of oatmeal and milk, and hied him through back streets to the campus.

He was *not* surprised to hear that there had been a rush the night before,—of course there was a rush every night. But everything else was a complete surprise. Nobody was hurt at the rush—blows were incidental and not essential. There were no mangled corpses strewed over the ground. The students did *not* play base ball during prayers, but, as a majority, paid strict attention. That evening two sophomores did visit him, inwardly swearing at the remoteness of his room,—to murder him? Dear me, no! To shake hands with him and ask him to the Y. M. C. A. meeting. Was he bored to death by subscription men? Hardly. Few had the endurance to travel to Land's End.

One man came and demanded—not fifty dollars for the crew, but twenty-five cents for the G. U. N. Algernon thought a case like this was "different," so he wrote to his father, received permission from him, and on the East Divinityite's second appearance promptly paid his subscription. Other requests for money he politely but firmly refused.

Was he hazed at all? · Well, yes. Rashly visiting the gym, he was seized by a band of sophomores, who, disgusted with his weakness and inanity, merely made him do obeisance and then kicked him out. A second time he found himself alive contrary to expectations.

Another great surprise was the athletics. He expected to hear of nothing else. As a matter of fact his companions talked of nothing but study, and when he went to buy his books he found a great crowd doing likewise, and but few at the cigarette counter. He had previously looked for the "bundle of books and four car-loads of cigarettes." and was now slowly realizing that his infallible *Sun* and *Herald* were really fallible.

Space forbids to tell of half his surprises, but any Yale man can tell that little Algernon went home to stay over his first Sunday with distrust of the New York papers, and the dawning of a genuine boyhood and manhood in his breast.

And Uncle Jim only laughed.

"JES A FEW MO' LEF'—'THOUT 'ZAGGERATION!"

A STRAY "LIT." ARTICLE.

AS flocks of birds fly northward in the spring, fly north with tireless wing day after day, so in the early days of fragrant June we walked with steady pace and northward too.

Side by side we tramped for days and days, looked at the world together, ate and slept in peace.

We walked through quiet villages and busy towns, through farming lands, by pasture lots and barns, past mills where millers ground the farmers' grist, o'er hills and dales, through woods, by roaring streams. The world was full of peace and love and joy; with it we were content.

At night we slept beneath some friendly tree; at daybreak on we jogged again. At noon we rested in some shady nook, but sunset found us on the road once more. And often, as we walked, we sang

"A merry heart goes all the day;
Your sad tires in a mile—a."

Two weeks thus glided by and with each day our joy increased.

One Sunday morning (it was the third), tired from a moonlight tramp the night before, we lay down in the long, sweet grass upon a river's bank; quite covered were we by the fragrant verdure, and as we there reposed the chestnut trees above us sprinkled all the ground with long, sweet blossoms.

Screened by sassafras and spicewood shrubs, whose fragrance mingled with the sweetly ladened breeze, we lay, and watched the sun sweep up the sky and heard the joyous matin of the birds grow faint and fainter till but now a chirp and then a twitter stirred the quiet air.

Before us, lying thus, there passed a maiden, clad in soft robes of flowing white. Loose was her hair and wavy as the grasses that gently murmured on the river's brink; kindly her smile as swiftly rose before her a golden robin, glorious as the sun; earnest her look as by the stream she paused; thoughtful the light that lay deep in her eyes; graceful her body as with ease unstudied she sank reclining on the mossy bank.

*   *   *   *

As here we sat we heard the rushing of another stream, which farther down received the waters of the brook that flowed before us.

"This brook," quoth I, "is like the gentle stream of your sweet life, which blesses all the fertile fields through which it flows and leaps the stony narrows to resume its peaceful course in broad and gentle curves,

That torrent yonder which we hear, impetuous toward its sources, but calmer here, and kind and plenteous down below—that stream which gathers in the waters of this brook and with them flows harmonious to the sea—can that be mine?"

"Perchance," quoth she, her head upon my arm.
"*May it?*" said I.
. "*It may.*"

THE SENIOR PROM.

A LUMNI, of my hopes the bane,
    How changed a garb thou hast to-night;
Instead of hall so dark and drear,
    Thou art a perfect blaze of light.

In you, so changed, I'd never see
    The dungeon dread I feared before;
Sweet Cupid now is warder where
    Grim Profs. and tutors walked of yore.

Yon corner, where I've often flunked,
    Now partly shields a spoony pair,
And round the hall, despair's abode,
    There trip gay youths and maidens fair.

Let those who can drain pleasure's cup,
 · But I, myself, could never, here
In this vile place, where I have had
    My pride so humbled twice a year.

I do believe, if I'd the cheek
    To mingle in merry rout,
The ghosts of my conditions large,
    Would rise and straightway drive me out.

A CHILD'S DREAM OF AN IDEAL FATHER.

A ND as I sat in the uncomfortable seat of the recitation, my soul was sore troubled and I slept. And as I slept I saw a vision. And lo! I dreamed that I was a happy youth with a bountiful sufficiency of where-with-all from my father. And as I dreamed it appeared that I e'en had the bulge on my fellow friends. For lo! *in primis*, my father did own a grand opera house in this city whereby I had a free pass to all the other theatres in the country. And I could see all the plays for nothing, while my companions e'en thought I was a blood. And also he was in the clothing busi ness so that I could get my variegated suits for a mere song, one suit for each day of the month, and I was adjudged a great swell. Then did a seventh uncle, three times removed die, and build a new dormitory which was labeled "Jones," leaving to his dear seventh nephew three times removed a free room on the second floor. And behold my father was also a railroad president, and I did have a free pass all over the country e'en to the uttermost parts of the earth. (This dream I dreamt before the passage of the Inter-State Commerce Act.) Then did it appear in the vision that some dear relative did own a beer foundry on which I had a strong "pull," and still another did run a champagne factory. Then did my father appear likewise to be a publisher and to fill several other useful functions of that sort. And at this point my sleep became troubled and methought I heard a voice call upon me by name. And it seemed very like unto the dulcet tones of the professor. And with a shudder I awoke and lo! it was a dream.

CIRCUMSTANCES ALTER APPEARANCES.

E.S.N.

THE DUDE THAT DIDN'T DANCE

I

I took my charming Dolly to the Senior Promenade,
I waltzed her 'round and treated her to punch and lemonade,
I whispered sweet and tender words whene'er I got a chance
But I'm sorry I introduced her to the Dude that didn't dance.

Chorus.;
I shall never forget my Dolly, I shall never forget her glance,
But I'm sorry I introduced her to the Dude that didn't dance.

II

I thought I would be foxy and monopolize her quite
For I didn't want another chap to waltz with her that night,
So I sought and found a man who couldn't waltz or even lance;
Now I'm sorry I introduced her to the Dude that didn't dance.

III

I waltzed with other partners then in old Alumni Hall
But Dolly's face and figure trim did far surpass them all;
I sauntered to the Chapel steps, but as I did advance
I saw her madly flirting with the Dude that didn't dance

IV

I led her to a corner dim and on the glassy floor
I knelt and vowed my burning love until my throat was sore,
She only smiled a cruel smile, and looked at me askance
Egad! She threw me over for the Dude that didn't dance

V

And now I mean to travel over every sea and land
A gatling gun upon my back, a bomb in either hand,
I mean to search in Ireland, in England and in France,
For I'm bound to find and massacre the Dude that didn't dance!

THE CHAPERONE.

A COMEDIETTA.

Dramatis Personæ:

MRS. VAN SLICK (Chaperone), a frisky widow in half mourning.
MISS EDITH MARSHMALLOW, } Her charges.
MISS CLARA VERE, }
MR. JACK DE LANCY, Yale '8—, Escort to Edith.
MR. TOM GILSEY, Same Class, Escort to Clara.
MR. J. STILTON ROQUEFORT, Athletic.
CENTER RUSH, Crew man.

SCENE I.—(Parlor of the New Haven House during hop.—Miss Marshmallow and Miss Vere discovered seated together, Mrs. Van Slick a little apart in a corner.)

De Lancy (introducing): Miss Marshmallow, let me present to you Mr. Roquefort, Miss Vere, Mr. Roquefort (aside to Edith), he's our great center rush, you know.

Roquefort (bowing): I am most happy to meet you, especially as I believe I am fortunate enough to have a dance with you at the Prom. to-morrow night.

Both Girls (together): Oh, Mr. Roquefort.

Roquefort: I am fortunate, I assure you.

Gilsey (in a whisper to Clara): He is a big gun, here, crew man.

Edith: Don't you play on the eleven, Mr. Roquefort?

Roquefort: I confess it, Miss Marshmallow, I played center rush last year.

Edith: O, how lovely! It must be awfully nice to play center rush.

Clara: And you row on the crew, don't you Mr. Roquefort?

Roquefort: I have the honor.

Clara: How nice! I do hope you'll beat Harvard next year.

De Lancy: This is our dance.

Edith: Oh, is it? (rises and takes his arm.) (Aside) He is perfectly lovely (casts a thrilling glance at Roquefort).

Gilsey: Shall we have a turn, Miss Clara?

Clara: O, yes. (Aside) He's too sweet for anything.

Roquefort: (turns away with an air born of many forms, glances idly about the room,—discovers Mrs. Van Slick seated alone).

Roquefort: (aside, surprised): Mrs. Van Slick, by Jove! (Advances toward her.) Oh, Mrs. Van Slick, this is an unexpected pleasure. I had no idea of finding you here.

Mrs. Van Slick (offering her hand): How do you do, Mr. Roquefort? I began to think you were not going to recognize me.

Roquefort: Really, Mrs. Van Slick, I only just saw

Mrs. Van Slick: Don't apologise—come now—confess you had forgotten me.

Roquefort (softly): Really, Mrs. Van Slick, you *know*

that would be impossible (aloud) but it was so unexpected—my finding *you* here.

Mrs. Van Slick: The unexpected, you know, is bound to happen. I am in here in no other position than as *chaperone* to the gay young buds who have just left us.

Roquefort: Chaperone! A new role I fancy (slyly), but tell me—in your new capacity have you quite forgotten Bar Harbor?

Mrs. Van Slick: Oh! that was so long ago. But, Sh! here come the young ladies. Say nothing of Bar Harbor before them.

Clara (flushed with the dance): Oh such a lovely dance, but so warm (drops Gilsey's arm). Mr. Roquefort, won't you take me into the corridor, I must have air.

Gilsey (aside): Her actions, at any rate, are decidedly cool.

Edith (aside): The bold thing. She treats Tom shamefully. Don't you think so, Mrs. Van Slick? Here they come back again. Oh, Mr. Roquefort, its so cool here. Won't you help me find my wrap. I think its on the stairs. (Exit with Roquefort.)

Clara (aside): The *audacity*. Really, Mrs. Van Slick, I think that pair needs you.

Tom and Jack (aside, together): Well, chappie, *we* were no use. (Enter Roquefort and Edith.)

Roquefort: Well, ladies, I must say good night. Training, you know.

Girls (in chorus): Don't forget my dance, Mr. Roquefort. Good night.

Roquefort: I shall be sure to remember them.

Girls (in chorus): Box 13, you know—Good night. (Aside) Ain't he perfectly stunning. (Exit with Tom and Jack.)

Roquefort: Good night, Mrs. Van Slick. We'll continue old times to-morrow night.

Mrs. Van Slick: Good night, Mr. Roquefort. Remember, not a word to the girls.

(Roquefort cast a quiek glance about the room and raises her hand to his lips.)

CURTAIN.

SCENE II.—At the Prom.—Box 13.—Somewhere in the Program.—Enter: Edith with De Lancy, Clara with Tom.

Edith: With Lander to play and a mile of crash to dance on, what could be more delightful!

Clara (aside): Mr. Roquefort to dance with.

Edith: I'm just crazy for the next waltz. Do I look all right, Mrs. Van Slick? Just shake out my back drapery again, please.

Clara: Oh! I am so nervous. *There*, I knew that *balayures* would tear out again. Hold my flowers, please, Tom, I beg pardon, Mr. Gilsey, while I pin it up. There; how's that?

De Lancy: Charming as always, Miss Vere. There,

see that sombre looking fellow there with the long hair. He's one of our notables. Funny editor of the *Courant*.

Gilsey to Edith: There's a fellow you ought to notice; he's the "young Webster" of the Yale assembly. There he goes—that one with the girl in green. That one behind him is Charlie Verituff. Richest man in Yale, and he's a stayer. Been here six years and a good show for a seventh.

Edith: Yes, yes, I see them, but my dress, I'm morally certain, it's ripped in the back. Oh! there's Mr. Roquefort at last. Doesn't he look handsome—and so strong! Let me see (consulting card), I have the 9th with him.

Clara: What's that crowd of men standing about the door for? They look as though they were lined up for a foot-ball rush.

De Lancy: That? Oh, that's the standing army of stags. They are waiting for intermission and ice cream.

Gilsey: Yes, and look out for your life and the front of your dress when their turn comes. They have no compunctions whatever against knocking a lady down for a plate of ice cream.

Girls in Chorus: How dreadful.

(The orchestra strikes up a waltz.)

Edith: There! There goes the music. Hurry, Mr. De Lancy. I wouldn't lose any of it for worlds; I'm just wild with excitement. Here, Mrs. Van Slick, please look out for my wraps, and, good-bye. Don't it make you wild to dance, too?

Clara: Oh! I'm so nervous. Please get off my feet, Mr. Gilsey. Oh, excuse me; it was only the chair leg.

There goes the rest of my balayures; but, never mind, it doesn't show. Here's my wrap, Mrs. Van Slick, I *wish* you were going to dance too. (They load Mrs. Van S. with wraps and disappear.)

Mrs. Van S. (with a sigh): Yes, I do wish I might dance. (Mr. Roquefort enters the box): How dye'do, again, Mr. Roquefort. Ah! you silly boy. Why ain't you dancing?

Roquefort: Simply because I prefer to sit here with you.

Mrs. Van Slick: But your partner. (Looking at his card.) You'r engaged for this dance. Look me in the eye, sir, and tell me—did you cut it?

Roquefort: With shame I confess it—I did. But you must admit I had provocation.

Mrs. Van Slick: Foolish fellow.

Roquefort: Not foolish, but fortunate; I can now talk with you.

Mrs. Van Slick: Ever a flatterer. You have lost nothing since Bar Harbor days.

Roquefort: Nothing but your company. You remember then how we used to go "rocking" together, or canoeing by moonlight. It was a happy time for me, Helen (with a sigh).

Mrs. Van Slick: Mrs. Van Slick, if you please. Were you as happy then as when strolling in the corridor last night?

Roquefort: Oh, that was by force.

Mrs. Van Slick: Or on the stairs?

Roquefort: Ah, I assure you I returned as quickly as I could. I thought of you always. (A moment's silence.)

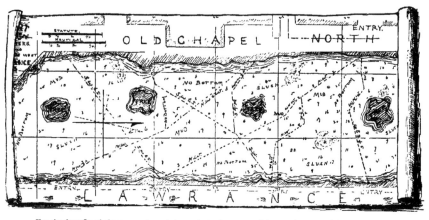

For the benefit of those accustomed to navigate the waters lying to the west of Lawrance the accompanying chart has been prepared—from soundings taken during the last thaw—at great expense by the *Record*.

Mrs. Van Slick: How well Lander plays to-night.

Roquefort: Yes. Do you remember how we used to dance together in the dining room at Rodick's?

Mrs. Van Slick: To be sure I do. How clumsy you were. You nearly crushed my feet one night.

Roquefort (aside): Confound it! She remembers too well. (Aloud) Really you are unkind; but I have improved since then. Would you like to try a turn?

Mrs. Van Slick: Oh, I don't know. Yes, I believe I should, just for the sake of old times. (She rises) No; not now; here are the girls. (Edith and Clara return with their escorts).

Roquefort (aside): Hang the luck!

Edith and Clara (in chorus): Oh, how do you do Mr. Roquefort? Isn't it just lovely here to-night?

Edith (in a whisper): I was just dying to have you come.

Clara (also in a whisper): I am anxiously looking for my dance with you.

Roquefort: I am delighted to see you again, ladies. Are you enjoying yourselves?.

Edith (with meaning): I am now.

Clara: Hugely; that is, I am beginning to.

Gilsey (to De Lancy): Always Roquefort.

De Lancy: I wish I had never introduced him.

Edith (examining her card): Why, Mr. Roquefort, just think: the next dance is ours.

Clara (examining her card): Why, Mr. Roquefort, isn't it splendid; the next is yours.

Roquefort: What! how is this? Surely I have not engaged the same dance with each of you.

Edith (showing her card): But I have you down.

Clara (showing her card): So have I.

Roquefort: There is some mistake here. Unfortunate mortal that I am, I have lost my card.

Edith: I am positive you had it with me.

Clara: I'm sure you had it with me.

(The girls glare at each other.)

Roquefort: But really, I can't dance with both of you.

Edith (magnanimously): You take it, Clara; you are the oldest.

Clara: No, you take it. Your card isn't full.

Edith (sharply): I have all I care for. Come, Jack; how could you be so stupid as to make a mistake. (They go on the floor).

Clara: I really couldn't take it from you. Come, Tom. (They join the promenaders).

Roquefort (soliloquizing): A slight interchange of feminine civilities (turning to Mrs. Van Slick): I am very sorry for the confusion; it was very fortunate (with a sly smile). Now *we* can have *our* dance.

Mrs. Van Slick: Oh, you wicked man!

(The orchestra begins a waltz and they disappear among the dancers.)

CURTAIN.

AT THE GERMAN.

SHE chose a little favor,
    And looked around the hall,
At last she hit upon a man
    Who stood against the wall;
She handed him the favor,
    He gave an eager start—
The fellow was a *stag* that night,
    The favor was a *heart.*

A STAG'S DIARY.

FEB. 2d.—It is now half-past four in the morning. Worn out by dancing and by my last struggles in the basement of the Armory, I have stumbled into my room, with another man's coat and hat, and have thrown myself into that same comfortable easy-chair, before the same dying embers, which I spoke of on January 11th. I went early to the Prom. and after frantic efforts I succeeded in getting three dances upon my card, and then retreated to the south end of the Armory, where, with a crowd of sympathizing stags and freshmen, I helped to obstruct the view of those who were unlucky enough to have seats near the entrance door. There I remained until the seventh dance, when a freshman staggered towards me with the remains of a straw in his mouth, and whispered to a classmate that there was some "red-colored stuff" in the corner room. Immediately I sneaked away from the stag's "stamping ground" and sought the source of the freshman's unsteadiness,—Lemonade. After the ninth intermission which I had with Miss Walzwell, my chum's girl, I took a position on the first step of the improvised dumb-waiter, deposited a silver dollar, and waited. One hour later I was handed a cup of "freshman tea" and a sandwich. I tried another dollar and another waiter. Twenty minutes more and he appeared bearing two plates of cream. A wild scramble ensued, during which my trousers fought well, for they carried away three-fourths of the cream. In dismay I sought to drown my wretchedness in the corner room. But there a prominent athlete doused my coat with a mixture of coffee, lemonade, and water. In this plight I lingered around until three A. M., appearing but twice upon the floor, once with Miss Heavytop, and once with Miss Shortstop, four feet tall. My back is better now! Thanks!

Finally I rushed to the basement where I encountered a confused mass of hats, gloves and coats. I determined to make an "exchange," and selected a new Dunlap hat, owner unknown. And now as I sit here before the above-mentioned embers, which are now dead, I do swear that I shall never again see the inside of the Meadow street barracks.

The Scientific Researches of our special artist in Composite Photography.

Our last Six Sweeps.

The Eleven's Feet.

Fourteen Subscription Fiends.

The Crew's Arms.

The Class of '92.

The Nine's Hands.

150 New Haven Landladies.

The New Haven Police Force.

"BLOOD WILL TELL."

ALONG the shadowed arbor-path
    Sweet Maud and I walked side by side,
In thoughtful mood: for in my heart
    A secret lurked I *must* confide.

I turned my passioned face to hers,
    And told my tale; then took her hand—
Her slender hand—in mine, and asked
    An answer fair to my demand.

No word she spoke; but all the blood
    Came rushing from her heart pell-mell,
And dyed her cheek a blushing " yes."
    Aye, true's the saying, " Blood will tell "!

JUNIOR ENGLISH.

CHAUCER.

LIFE.—Descended from progenitors who, though endowed with but the merest trifle of this world's possessions, were yet opulent in that assemblage, and conglomeration of virtue denominated honesty. He flashes forth in the history of English literature, as the meteor in its parabolic orbit, cleaving the darkness of the midnight sky, streams in a gorgeous trail of luminosity across the firmament; and then expires in the void of nothingness, only to render the darkness more visible. During his collegiate course, he spent much of his time on horse-back, and many an hour would he spend galloping along on his favorite steed, perusing Harper's Editor of Homer—hence his love of poetry. A green old age was entwining him in its verdant embrace, when grim-visaged death stretched forth his bloodless hand, and plucked him from the earth. Appended to the funeral notice in the daily press was this touching reminder of his own composition :

    " When to mi grave mi way I wende,
    I beg mi freendes ne flowres to sende."

APPEARANCE.—A short man of considerable height, his black eyes flashing from their azure depths beneath the straight brown hair clustered in ringlets about his highly narrow forehead.

STYLE.—Terse, voluble, flowing, turgid, fresh, original, animated, grand, majestic, simple, unpretending, flexible, harmonious, easy, vigorous, cramped, irksome, studied, labored, unnatural, graceful.

RANK.—Highest of the high, he has made rapid strides of progression, leavening the alliterative schools of poets of the " Rum, Romanism and Rebellion " sort far in the rear. Of him, in very truth could the Glee Club sing :

" First in Peace, first in War, first in the hearts of his
    countrymen. '

CHARACTER.—To discover the definition for so unprecedented a combination of attractions, is attended with great difficulty. At once joyous and morose, he was more sweet than the gentle southwest wind ; yet the gall of the freshman in his annual sour on the Promenade could not equal his bitter acidity.

INFLUENCE.—Unprecedented, unsurpassed and un-surpassable. Still it was less than, under the circumstances it should have been, and not so tremendously extensive, as in our own age, where its strength is particularly felt in the orthography.

SHAKESPEARE.

LIFE.—When Mrs. Shakespeare presented Willie to Mr. S. and the world, a close observer might have clearly discerned a ripple rising on the sea of English literature, which broadened, heightened and deepened, till it swelled into a mighty billow of unapproachable grandeur, o'ertopping the foamy waves of microscopic magnitude, overwhelming animate and inanimate nature in its track, till with thundering sound it breaks upon the strand, and still rushing, seething on leaves its snowy foam-mark high on the shore of time. As his name, with slight etymological changes, would seem to indicate he shook himself out of his original sp(h)ere at an early stage in his existence ; and existed thereafter on the stage. He discovered by some intuitive instinct, that he could write good plays, and was a right good plagiarist, too. No agonizing Soph., struggling in the toils of a composition, could utilize more readily, thoroughly or successfully the subject matter of antecedent writers. A life of matrimonial infelicity, (too many actresses about) terminated in the grave, when, having " shuffled off this mortal coil,"—the last hand—he showed aces up to the other fellow's three twos, and passed in his chips for good.

WORKS.—It is now the well-nigh universal opinion that he did not write at least half the plays usually attributed to him, and that some one else wrote the other half.

STYLE.—Graceful, unnatural, labored, studied, irksome, cramped, vigorous, easy, harmonious, flexible, unpretending, simple, majestic, grand, animated, original, fresh, turgid, flowing, voluble, terse.

INFLUENCE.—Surpassingly enormous, as was his influence on the literature of all succeeding time ; it is, in a great degree belittled and counter-balanced by the evil moral influence which he exerts on later generations. He put the stage on its legs, or vice versa, thereby encouraging the wicked, wicked theater, and leading astray susceptible youths.

Stereotyped and Abridged Form for the Recitation room. Warranted to suit all classes and conditions of writers.

LIFE.—Was born, married wrong woman, had a hard time of it, and died in poverty. *Works.*—It is well to make slight variations under this head. *Style.*—Good. *Rank.*—High. *Character.*—Good. *Influence.*—Great.

A Troubadour wooing a damosel fair,
Was telling his passionate love,
When he saw a white handkerchief waved in
                                    the air
From a parapet high up above:
"Ah, had I the wings!"—
            he yearningly sings—
"Ah, had I the wings of a dove!"

But a rope-ladder
        soon to his
sight was displayed.
And he eagerly climbed to the top,
Where, instead of beholding the beauteous
                                        maid,
He was warmly received by her Pop—
And with horror, he hears
            the clicking of shears
And a half of the rope-ladder drop!—

"I'll teach you—rash villain—my daughter to woo
To the dungeon!—Ho-warder I say!"
So in spite of entreaties
        and all he could do
He was roughly conducted
                away—
And unless he got out,
        I haven't a doubt
He remains in his cell to this day!

MY CHUM'S SISTER.

OFTEN times when I am conning,
    Something that I just detest,
(And I own I find all studies,
    Stupid at the very best);
Then my eyes are ever turning
    To your sweet and peaceful face,
And I dream—oh, heavenly rapture,
    That I hold your brother's place.

You must be my guiding angel,
    For, when I look at you, I see
Your soft eyes ever are exerting
    Some good influence on me.
How I wish you were my sister!
    Chummie might dispense with you,
For, alas, I haven't any,
    And he says that he has two.

Happy thought! It might be managed,
    A la mode of now-a-days,
For, they say, 'tis but a poor rule
    That you cannot work both ways;
If, when you have known me longer,
    I should ask you if you'd be,
Something more than friend or cousin,
    Perhaps a sister unto me,
Will you not then answer blushing
    " I will trust you with my life;
I can never be your sister,
    But—I'll always be your wife!"

"THE TUTOR, MR. BARLOW."

"MY DEAR SANDFORD," said Mr. Barlow, laying down a book which he had been reading, "would you and Merton like to go down town with me this afternoon?" Sandford looked across the table, at which they were seated, at Merton ; then, after kicking him slyly, they both replied in chorus : "Dear Mr. Barlow, it is yours to command us in any way which may contribute to your happiness." " Then," said Mr. Barlow, "as you should have furnished your allotted tasks ere this, you may put on your caps and rubbers, and I will await you in the hall, as I must first take my tonic." " Ah, that reminds me," said Merton, "Can you tell me, my dear instructor, what S. O. P. stands for on the label of your tonic, as Sandford and myself feel compelled to express our ignorance?" Mr. Barlow blushed, not in confusion at the question, but more in pity for his pupil, (at least, this was the only reason suggested to Merton's mind,) and replying, said : "Why, my dear child, didn't you know that S. O. P. stands for the size of a bottle, and means in the present instance somewhat over a pint?" " Thanks," said Sandford and Merton. Mr. Barlow still blushed as they started forth; Sandford and Merton remarking, "What a nice time we're having," walked stolidly on.

As they passed a clothing establishment, Sandford silently and surreptitiously took a placard from off a model's back, which read : "Goods slightly damaged by the late fire. Immense sacrifice." And still acting in a somewhat absent-minded manner, affixed the afore-mentioded placard to Mr. Barlow's back. As the streets were somewhat crowded, the people, attracted by Merton's laughter, turned around, and seeing the placard, in their turn commenced first to smile, then to jeer.

Finally, Mr. Barlow was compelled to ask his pupils if they knew the cause of the people's laughter. Sandford meekly replied that his clothes were not as good as Merton's, and were so old-fashioned that the people were laughing at him. Merton, aghast at his answer, placing his hand behind Mr. Barlow's back to withdraw the placard and expose Sandford's treachery, was caught by Mr. Barlow as he was pulling the crooked pin from his coat. Mr. Barlow looked at Sandford, who, bursting into tears, gave free reins to his grief. Mr. Barlow was amazed. "Why this grief, my dear Sandford?" he said. "Ah, sir," said Sandford, "as this is the first time Merton has ever been caught, I beseech you to spare my dear friend and fellow schoolmate." Merton, overcome with indignation at Sandford's perfidy, commenced to explain, but, like poor Mr. Bultitude in "Vice Versa," was not permitted to do so. "You may both, on your return home,"

SAY, boss want a shine?
 What! Aint got the time?
I'll guv yer this rosebud, and shine 'em up
  doodle.
Aw come, boss, I'll match ye,
Ha! knowed that I'd catch ye,
  Put yer foot on the growler, I'll trust fer the
  boodle.

Buy a paper this mornin,? the dindiest lot;
Yer can't name a paper wot I haven't got!
A "Sun?" Well, de Yaleses beat yist'day, they
  say,
And there aint no account in that paper terdsy.
A "World"? All sold out. Well, then wot hev
  I got?
Jes' one "Register" left. `Say, boss buy out de
  lot!

THE STREET URCHIN.

said Mr. Barlow, "repeat orally to me, in hexameter verse, the story of the ' Thirsty Cormorant and the Benighted Plumber.' I impose this slight punishment as you are probably both to blame. You might produce something on a par with the following verse:

> "We pray the Muse us to enlighten,
>   Concerning this plumber all benighten,
> Who, thus far away from all his aunts,
>   Will soon be eaten by the Cormorants."

Sandford and Merton having correctly copied this down upon their cuffs, thanked their kind tutor.

In their progress they saw two personages who by their appearance were attracting universal attention. As they approached their faces seemed strangely familiar to Mr. Barlow, but as the hats which these personages wore almost concealed their features, it was not possible to distinguish them at a distance; however, as they came nearer, Mr. Barlow exclaimed in a quiet, suave manner, "I knew I couldn't be mistaken, being a tutor. Uncle George and Rollo, permit me to introduce my scholars, Sandford and Merton." Uncle George and Rollo, after glancing at their guide books to see if any such persons were enrolled therein, bowed humbly. "It gives us pleasure to meet you, one and all," they said in union. "Will you join us in our study of human nature?" asked Mr. Barlow. "But," he added, "before we proceed further, will you

inform me, merely as a disinterested spectator, why you and Rollo wear such old hats?" Uncle George seemed somewhat astonished at first at this query; he had not just cause to be so, inasmuch as he wore a hat which was surmounted with a sugar loaf crown, and Rollo appeared in his inevitable cap with a tassel, not a "tassle," as Rollo's was peculiarly a "tawsle." "The fact is," said Uncle George, "that Rollo and I determined to wear the same hat through one trip, as we only stay one day in each place we cannot purchase any suitable hats, inasmuch as the hat which is fashionable in the East would be laughed at in the West; accordingly Rollo has calculated that if we refrain from purchasing new hats, we can both subscribe to the *Gospel Union News*, which is too great an inducement to be lost."

As Uncle George said these words, Rollo drew a large piece of foolscap from his pocket, but before he could commence to explain his figures, Mr. Barlow leaped nimbly on a passing horse car, and called out to his pupils, "I leave you to listen to Rollo's statistics. You had better walk home, as you know I have all your ready money, and don't be late to your lessons." Mr. Barlow's last words were hardly distinguishable as the car passed around a corner and bore him out of sight, leaving Uncle George, Rollo, Sandford and Merton gazing at each other in blank amazement.

ON HAND-SHAKING.

I MET a friend in front of South to-day;
A fortnight, more or less, he'd been away,
And I, that I might seem as, truth, I felt,
A little glad that still on earth he dwelt,
Stretched forth my hand his wandering palm to take
Within my own, for one good cordial shake,
My Queen! what log, what lifeless stick of wood
Did I receive in place of flesh and blood !
I tried to squeeze, to wring, to shake, to press,
But there it hung—a thing of life, life-less.
I squoze until the limp joints snapped for pain
And then I tried to shake them well again.
But vain the task and vain was my alarm,
As well have tried to shake a lever arm.
A pump, when worked, will give some answering sign
That springs of feeling dwell within its shrine,
But though I worked this handle with a will
I could not rou:e a solitary thrill.
O blest be he who shakes with all his soul
And curst be he who makes you do the whole.

A NEW DORMITORY.

WE have the pleasure to announce to our friends that
the funds for a new dormitory have been promised to the college. The promising has been done on
the condition that some second party will do the giving.
If the second party is as ready to come forward as the
promisor has been, we may be assured that another
handsome building will loom up on the campus at no
distant day. It is designed, however, for the " cops."
For many years it has been a student problem what to
do with the " cops." We almost wonder that a pam-
phlet has not appeared upon " What to do with our
' cops '?" by the author of " What to do with our
boys?" etc. They have been enticed from place to
place about the campus and exposed to dynamite fiends
and the inclemencies of the weather. The corner of
Durfee has been their lurking place, and their billies
have not been safe within their hands. Their night
watches have worn upon them, and they have longed
for a quiet beat in an uptown quarter, where occasional
naps and a swig at the corner grocery might refresh
them. But the new dormitory has done away with all
these difficulties. To describe the plans in full would
weary our pen and your patience. Through the kind-
ness of the architect we were allowed to inspect a portion of his designs. As they are not yet fully matured,
however, we can only give a general idea of their nature
to our readers.

It is designed to have the building of brick, taken
from the old brick row for association's sake. It will
be circular in form, and will be situated in the center of
the campus, which will be in the form of a hollow
square or quadrangle. The dormitories of the students
will be situated about the four sides of this quadrangle,
and the front of each room will consist of a single window of plate glass. In a revolving tower which will
surmount the central dormitory, a telescope will be
mounted, which may be brought to bear upon any of

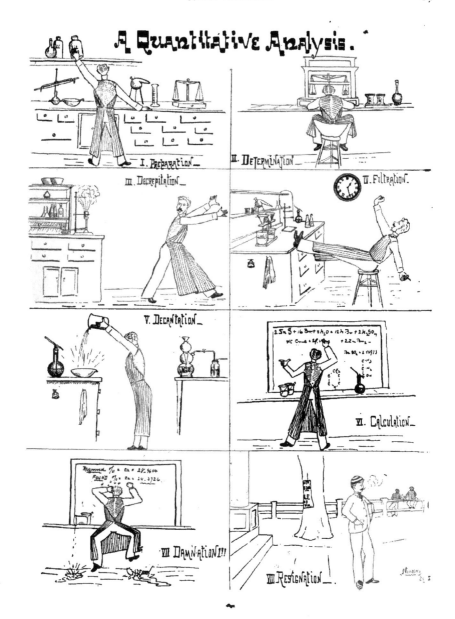

these rooms at pleasure. The obvious advantage of this method for the detection of any miscreants needs no further explanation. The building itself will be surrounded by a moat, which at night may serve as a means of protection, and by day will afford convenient opportunities for practicing the aquatic arts. Further cries for bath-rooms will be unnecessary, as the moat will be an admirable substitute. If any become dissatisfied with its facilities, they will be referred to the old saying about plucking the beam from your own eye before plucking the mote from your neighbors.

The arrangement for extinguishing campus fires will be novel as well as original. In a turret above the observatory tower a mortar will be placed with a quantity of fire-grenades at hand. At the first appearance of fire in any direction, it will be signalled from the tower to the turret above, where a brave minion of the law will be ready to bombard it with fire-grenades until it is extinguished. This will prevent all danger from infernal machines, and will save the wear and tear of sole-leather, as well as exposure to the damp night air.

The ventilators of all the student's rooms will be connected by an ingeniously contrived telephonic apparatus with a receiving machine in the main office of the central dormitory. Here all conversations and disturbances will be recorded by a self-acting phonograph, to be used as future evidence in the city courts.

For fire-places, an admirable device has been adopted. They will be situated in the doorways, where all peanut venders and apple boys will be fired in the heat of indignation.

There is but one more feature of the building to be noticed. The occupants of these elaborate quarters will become so puffed up with their own importance and the elegance of their surroundings, that no forms will be good enough for them to look upon except their own. To afford them ample opportunity for this admiration of themselves, numerous mirrors will be placed about the building and its hallways. Before these mirrors, hourly squad drills will be held, and though dynamite has failed, the enormity of their own conceit will surely succeed in blowing them up at last.

We will go no further into the details of the project. Enough has been said to arouse the interest of the students. The only thing necessary for its successful completion is the promised funds. A list will be placed for signatures at Beers'. In view of the worthiness of the object and the possibility of the final eradication of the campus trespassers, it will probably not succeed.

RONDEAU.

M Y love (alas, she is my love
    In no possessive sense,)
Said: "Sir, I saw you gaze upon
    Another maid too tenderly;
Is *that* all that you care for me ?"
    (Well, here's a pretty mess!)

Whilst I, with tender gaze and sigh,
    Protest my love does never die;
Yet dare not say in repartee:
    "How, then, about those young men three
To whom you fly when each you see;
    Is *that* all that *you* care for *me* ?"
        (Alas, she might say "yes!")

A "CHIP"—FROM AN ANCIENT TABLET.

[EVIDENTLY DRAWN FROM "LIFE."]

WASHINGTON'S BIRTHDAY.

THE TAILOR!

WHO fills whole columns in the press?
       The tailor!
Makes offers such as none could guess?
       The tailor!
Who advertises patterns new,
Invites you all to come and view,
What bargains he will make for you?
       The tailor!

Who sends round notes, petite and rare?
And makes our postman fume and swear?
       The tailor!
Who cuts his prices. Oh, so low!
Takes ten per cent. off, still you know,
Because he loves the student so?
       The tailor!

Who, when you call, begins to smile?
       The tailor!
And shows you every earthly style?
       The tailor!
Who says, he would your order fill,
And if you choose to run a bill,
Can give you all the time you will?
       The tailor!

Who just the same, sends round his man?
       The tailor!
And makes just all the fuss he can!
       The tailor!
Who, when your funds are wholly spent,
To threat'nings dire gives fullest vent,
And has the bill to your father sent?
       The tailor!

FROM ADVANCE SHEETS.

[*To the Editors of the* YALE RECORD.

DEAR SIRS:—We take great pleasure in forwarding you advance sheets of our new book, "The Complete College Letter Writer; or, The Undergraduate Vade Mecum." Hoping that it will receive favorable notice in your columns,
       We are respectfully,
              —— ——]

[Letter from a young man who has been suspended, to his father, whom he wishes to keep in ignorance of the fact.]

My dear Father:—I am happy that I am able to give you a most satisfactory answer to your inquiries as to my studies. Prof. X—— has been detailed by the Faculty to observe certain meteorological phenomena now occurring near Milford, in this state, and incidentally he will examine the geological formations and the flora of that region.

Prof. X—— has selected me to accompany him and to be his assistant on the trip. It will involve considerable extra work in addition to my regular studies, but the honor and the opportunities for acquiring information are great. Of course it will require a check to defray expenses of journey. My address will be Milford, Conn. My probable stay will be six weeks.
       Your affectionate son,
              HARRY N——.

[From a young man under temporary financial embarrassment, to a furniture dealer in answer to an urgent demand for payment.]

Dear Sir:—I am sorry to have caused you any inconvenience by my slight delay in settling my bill, and I feel that the least I can do is to give you some reparation in increased patronage. You therefore may send to my address, 1192 Durfee, the rose-wood cabinet now in your show-window, a couch and arm-chair to match, and charge to my account.
       Very truly,   TOM T——.

[From a washwoman, who desires an advance of money.]

Mr. J——,

dear sir:—i am in trouble; my youngest son yesterday fell down stairs breaking his leg, and the grocer has sent in his bill, and please send five dollars by bearer and bridget maginness will pray for your soul.

[Answer to preceding.]

Mrs. Maginniss,

Dear Madam:—It it with deep distress that I hear of your fresh affliction. This is even more the case because my conscience tells me that, alas! I am not free from blame.

When I first engaged you six months ago you were the head of a happy and healthy family of fourteen children and had a cheerful and obedient assistant in your husband. But I was the evil genius. Scarce a week had passed ere your eldest son, Patrick, was thrown from a cart and injured his back; ten days later Mary was torn by a fierce dog; within a fortnight Bessie was married. These were but the beginnings of a chain of misfortunes. Luckily but three have died so far, but I feel there is a fatality connected with my wash and you have suffered more than your share from it. You need not call for my clothes next week.

I will not remind you of the sums I have advanced from time to time and for which you are in my debt. I know it would be useless—your gratitude is so great. Henceforth our paths lie apart.
       Sadly,   Henry I——.

[From a romantic young man to a young woman ditto.]

Dear Bess:—Meet me by moonlight, alone. Y——k Square. Eight o'clock.

(Signed). [Any name but the right one].

SLEIGHING.

OWN in the dingle,
The sleigh bells jingle;
My fingers tingle
    Through gloves of fur.
Thus onward flitting,
The crisp crust splitting,
I'm happy sitting
    Here close to her.

The moon shines brightly.
My steed is sprightly;
And pulls, not lightly,
    The leathern strands.
Though I to stop her
Don't care a copper,
Yet, since it's proper,
    I use both hands.

The moon, high riding,
As downward sliding;
Soon she'll be hiding
    Behind that bluff.
With nothing binding,
And no one minding,
Then I'll be finding
    One hand enough.

TO WHOM IT MAY CONCERN.

IT is really wonderful to what a degree of uncon-
cern as to his surroundings a man can come, merely
by living in the old brick row. He takes up his abode
in one of those venerable buildings, presumably an
ordinary mortal; in less than a week he has become a
monster of apathy and indifference, and retains this
character as long as he dwells there. It is a wise pro-
vision of nature that he can adapt his nervous system
as he does, for otherwise it would be ruined by the experiences of a single night. I shall never forget my
first attempt to sleep in college. Not that anything
very much out of the usual way occurred in the building that night, but I was inexperienced, and, as one
strange sound after another reached my ears, a vague
feeling of alarm soon increased to a perfect panic. In
the morning I fully expected to hear that some dark
deed had been done in the gloom of the night, but no
one referred to it in the remotest way. I furtively ex-
amined the morning papers, but there was no mention
of midnight violence. Very differently the old inhab-
itants view the cries and noises of day and night.
They experience no uneasiness at the jingle of breaking glass, accompanied by shouts and groans, for they
have learned to know that it all means no more than
a friendly scrimmage, the consequences of which will
likely be no worse than a bill for broken window panes.
They do not start at the crack of pistols in the entry,
for probably it is only the sophomores on the top floor
improvising a shooting gallery. Scuffling of feet,
sounds of blows, and cries of "slug him," are but
signs of a little bout of the manly art which is going

on somewhere near. Agonized wails and footsteps on the stairs suggest to them no ghostly visitant, but merely the entry tenor; and when a woman's pleading tones are wafted through their coal closets, they recognize the lady who contracts for their neighbor's washing. Not only do these men attach no importance to such manifestations, but such is the adaptability of the human mind to its surroundings that they soon cease to hear them altogether. Should I happen to hear one of my classmates in mortal agony just outside my door, though probabilities are greatly in favor of my not hearing him, I doubt whether the fact would have enough influence on me to make me investigate the cause of his outcry. Naturally, I am sympathetic in the extreme, but long residence in the brick row has made me what I am. In thinking over this peculiar aspect of life on the campus the other day, I was struck with the thought of what wonderful advantages the halls of the older dormitories offer to assassins, garroters, and others contemplating lawless deeds of a like nature. If the intended victim can once be enticed within the doors of any building in the brick row, his doom is sealed. No cries will rouse the dwellers, no sound of blows will betray the character of what is going on. Murder under such circumstances cannot fail to be a complete success. Now I am not a murderer myself, nor would I encourage murder in the least, so I do not elaborate the idea further; but I think it no more than fair to make the statement I have just made, for the benefit of those who are looking for some safe and convenient place to commit murder in, as well as a warning to agents, old-clothes dealers, duns and others, who have reason to suspect their fellow-mortals of wishing them out of the way. I trust my motives will meet the appreciation which I think they deserve.

O, FICKLE LOVE.

AT eve they stood upon the quay,
   The sun's red disk was sinking in the sea,
    His hands clasped hers as tight could be,
Their lips were, oh, so near.

Her grief she did not try to hide.
   They kissed. He clambered up the steamer's side;
    "Wait for me, love," he softly cried,
" If only for a year."

But since that eve they've never met,
   The world is wide, lovers their vows forget;
    Do they remember, think you, yet
That kiss upon the pier?

UNANIMITY.

Ethel: Yes, indeed, Yale has turned out many good men !

Jack (who has recently been expelled), with feeling : Ah, I agree with you perfectly on that point.

MODERN DRESS.

RONDEAU.

DAN Cupid's in a sorry plight
    He's stabbed a maid with all his might,
And weeping, stands with eyes turned low,
(Like woman, when her lovers go)
And mourns his ill success, I trow.

"The reason?" begs a maid of Greece,
"Without Love's reign the world must cease!"
A fantasy of long lost Peace
        And Acadie.

The reason's plain, poor maid, I said,
A dance degenerate Fashion's led.
A maiden now on thoroughfare
The arrow's prick can safely dare;
And thank—her clever corsetlére!

HE USED IT.

"Why, Jack, what on earth's the matter?"

Jack (who has played his first game): "Nothing! Only, you see, I heard those players saying that success in foot ball depended a good deal on a fellow's using his head."

THE COLLEGE SYMPHONY.

I USED to wonder what my destiny would be, and at times I would speculate and imagine myself a member of one of the three learned professions, and would grow melancholy, as I pondered over my unfitness for any one of them. That is all changed now. I am destined, on leaving college, to study harmony, counterpoint, and composition, and my *magnum opus* will be a symphony in four movements, representing four years of a college course.

I shall begin with a passage on the 'cellos, slow, majestic and dignified, representing the "I own the earth" feeling of a freshman, on passing his examinations. This will grow gradually into a hesitating, timid strain, representing his feelings on his arrival in town. Then a martial motive, the freshmen going to the rush, culminating in a grand crash and uproar, for which I shall use the entire orchestra. "The freshman march" motive will then be taken up by the flutes, with an undercurrent of "Oh, fresh, put out that light!" done by the drums. The examination motive will ensue, the yell of the youths as they rush for seats in Alumni Hall, and then a confused murmur, representing the perplexity of the freshman over his first examination paper, which gradually, by slow degrees, straightens out into a more cheerful strain, as, having conquered the paper, he hands it, with a triumphant smile, to the instructor in charge, and goes forth to a confused jumble of "What did you get for the fifth problem?—" "where in thunder is my"—"got a cigarette about your"—"give me a light, for goodness"—"Jones says he flunked the"—"when the Glee Club comes to"—"what is the first train for"—"I climbed his frame and jumped on his"—"Thompson's the biggest chump I ever"—

In the midst of this the chimes ring out dinner-time, and the crowd separates, for the last meal of the term in New Haven.

The "promenade motive" will then be taken up by the brass instruments, accompanied by a plaintive twitter of the violins, representing the dissatisfaction of the freshmen at not being allowed to dance. Close upon this will follow "Banger day," represented by the cornets and trombones. A descriptive passage will ensue, representing the breaking up of winter. Soon after we shall see the freshman nine in combat with Harvard. The "fence motive" will follow, in the midst of which the Junior Society songs will be heard in the distance, while the freshmen look on from the fence, and wonder how it will feel when their turn comes. The "examination motive" will again be heard in the distance, coming nearer and nearer, and we shall again hear the freshmen yell as they rush after seats. The tramp, tramp, tramp, of the tutor will be heard, as he moves up and down, and the confused murmur will be repeated, working up to a shout of joy as the freshman finally leaves Alumni Hall to find himself a sophomore.

This is as far as I have gone in the scheme for my symphony. The second, third and fourth movements I shall work up as soon as possible. I think no one will doubt that I have a glorious future before me.

WITH A BOX OF CANDY.

"A CURE for 'blues'" you asked of me,
        Sweet lady; so I sought among
The doctor's books; but naught did see
Of remedy for that sad ill,
Until, while glancing o'er a page
Of homoeopathic work, my eye
Read eagerly this sentence sage;
"Like cures like." So here's your cure,
Which is as sweet as sweets can be;
And so, dear lady, like to thee.

AT THE GAME.

Edith : Is that dreadfully little man below the famous pitcher?

Dorothy : Yes, dear, but do take care or he will overhear. You
know little pitchers have very big ears.

GEOLOGICAL METAPHYSICS.

AWAY back in the early ages of the world, before the brick row had been commenced, or
Homer had commenced his poems for the freshmen, a
host of little Rhizopods were sporting on the shores of
the new-made ocean. The ocean was young then and
fresh and the Rhizopods bathed twice a day at the rising of the tide, and never had a thought for the mor-
row or the changing fashions. Their only occupations
were the pleasures of the shore and—but I am wandering from the subject.

The long stretches of moonlit beach were visited at
times by another being, at least history speaks of it as
a being, although no psychologist was present at the
time to determine its entity or nonentity. It was an
Ego, which during the warm summer months flitted
down to the shore to get a whiff of the ocean breeze
and hold sly flirtations with the little Rhizopods. It
was not an ordinary Ego, but a large and handsome
specimen clothed in a capital E and a diamond shirt
stud. All the little Rhizopods were madly in love with
it, and why should they not be ; for what else was there
upon which they might bestow their affections except
the dancing wavelets which kissed their pink-hued
cheeks, and the magnificent presence of the Ego? Nor
was the Ego averse to their attentions. It wandered

over the vast solitudes of the continents with a listless semi-conscious air until it met the little Rhizopods and then all was mirth and gladness. The Rhizopods sported with the Ego, and in time were caressed by the wavelets on the sly. There was nothing to disturb their dream of happiness.

But one day a stranger found its way to the shore, another lonely wanderer seeking society of its kind. It was a nonentity and answered to the name of a Non-Ego, a pretty, pert Non-Ego, which wore a hyphen for a necktie and could charm a Dodo with its smile. It did charm the Ego. No sooner had the Ego seen the airy graces of the sweet Non-Ego, than the little Rhiz-opods were deserted and forgotten. Nothing was so pleasing to it as to bask in the sunshine of the Non-Ego's smiles. They played together, sang together, sketched together. The moonlight found them upon the rocks above the sea, telling to each other their tale of love; and in the morning they wandered far inland or visited the museum where the mastodon and the ichthyosaurus were displayed.

The poor bewildered little Rhizopods! At first they talked and wondered and could not comprehend. But soon the whole truth flashed upon them and jealousy turned their hearts to stone. They were changed into the rocky cliffs along the shore. The sparkling waves still caressed them tenderly, but meeting with the cold repulses of their stony hearts, in fury they lashed the defenceless heads of the little Rhizopods, and wore deep furrows in their cheeks, down which trickled the tears of disappointment. But the Ego and Non-Ego, they thought not of the Rhizopods and the waves. The intensity of their love absorbed them both until they became united and formed a human soul, with a theorizing psychologist ever tagging at its ever receding heels. And the Rhizopods, they are still on the shore, but no attentions now are paid to them except by some stray geologist who carelessly gathers them up and places them in his cabinet, little thinking of the veil of romance which surrounds their early lives.

REFLECTIONS

ON THE PORTRAIT OF ELIHU YALE ON THE "LIT" COVER.

POOR old Elihu! Tackled for another subscrip-tion! I know exactly what you are about to say as you stand there defiantly with your hand on your hip. "No sir, not another penny! I have given all I intend to that country college I never expect to see!"

That scroll on the table near you is undoubtedly some dunning letter containing a plan of the proposed college building drawn by some aspiring New Haven artist.

I can imagine about what they've said, Elihu. I've been there myself in a slight degree. I don't blame you at all for the indignant look you wear. Who knows but that you have been pestered and pursued by these specimens of the genus subscription man which now flourishes so luxuriantly in this same college which you fostered, even to your residence in London.

I haven't the faintest doubt that at each knock at the door you looked cautiously out of the window to see whether it was one of fiends or no, and on the slightest suspicion retired expediously into a closet or hastily crawled under the bed (ingenious tactics which have been followed by many generations of students since), only to reappear with bedraggled wig and dusty small clothes when you were assured that your tormentors had departed, balked of their prey.

But they've caught you this time, Elihu! There's no getting away from that letter. Pretty low way of striking a man that, through the mail. Your feelings can better be imagined than described.

What saith the poet?

" Murder a man's family and he may brook it,
But keep your hands out of his breeches pocket."

Yes, Elihu, you are in an unfortunate predicament, very unfortunate. Your very look betokens the nature of your thoughts.

What else can that aggrieved expression of indig-nant surprise indicate but "tackled for another sub-scription?"

How long you pondered remaining in this beligerent attitude, which the artist has so faithfully portrayed, tradition does not state, but since we learn that you gave various amounts at several different times to the embryo University, you probably ended by taking your seat with a weary sigh putting yourself down for — pounds, devoutly hoping they would never call for it.

AT THE MASQUERADE.

He—Is it all right when everything is masking,
　　Since people are not what they seem to-night,
　　Perhaps to flirt and to do so without asking,
　　　　Is it all right?

She—Is it all right when none can see your blushes,
　　Hearing sweet words you know full well are
　　　　light,
　　Yet to forget that doubt which ever crushes,
　　　　Is it all right?

He—Is it all right when no one will betray you,
　　(What lips half-seen do more than half invite,)
　　To steal one kiss—just one—confess, I pray you,
　　　　Is it all right?

She—Is it all right that after you have kissed her,
　　To say the least a thing most impolite,
　　She should unmask and say, "Since I'm your
　　　　sister,
　　　　Is it all right?"

A young lady en route to Florida, snowed up in New Haven, was visited by 150 students.—*Morning News.*

ITS AN ILL WIND, ETC.

THE "RECORD" SERIES OF TEXT-BOOKS.

WE have determined to join hands with the Co-operative Association in browbeating and crushing out high-priced monopoly from New Haven trade. We desire to lift up the down-trodden student and emancipate his pocketbook. To accomplish our high ideas and lofty aspirations, we print in this issue a text-book on Geology for the use of the Junior class. Psychologies are published in the same form. We would reprint Shakespeare for the benefit of the English division, but only literature of the first order can appear in the columns of the *Record.*

GEOLOGY.

Geology is the science of rocks. We all want rocks, we all admire the man of rocks, and not one of us would kick if our pockets were lined with mineralogical petrification. From the time when we were rocked in our cradles, through the boyish stages of the rocking horse, to the rocker of old age, we are eager in our pursuit of rocks. Geology teaches us of the composition of rocks, and may therefore throw some light on the method of disintegrating (popularly known as crushing) the hardest of all substances, the stony heart of a maiden. Altogether geology will prove an interesting study to all who have not been, during the winter, unwisely forced into an abrupt and distasteful acquaintance with the lithological structure of the pavements.

Rocks are made of sand and mud. Of these substances we already know something, there being a particularly large deposit of the former in New Haven, while samples of the latter have kindly been provided by a school in New Jersey. Historical geology most interests the observant student.

I. Archæn Time.—At this time one might have seen the naturally festive little Protozoans skipping about, hand in hand, with the first-born for a crossing to Beers' while the more learned and sedate Kizopocts, with due solemnity, founded Φ B. K., but their vanity was too much for them, they left their coats unbuttoned, caught cold, died, and the world passed on.

II. Tilurian Age.—Here we find more old friends, fossilized gag on the Rink deeply embedded in Paleozoic meters; the Chaucerian verse of our esteemed contemporary and the first birthdays of some of New Haven's fairest.

. III. Carboniferous Age.—In this age amidst the luxuriant vegetable growth which in its state of decay is making millionaires of New Haven coal dealers, the waving chestnut first flourished. Some of the fruit of the original tree is still preserved and distributed among the readers of our daily press.

IV. Reptilian Age.—It was in this age of reptiles, that the Archæanicus Brodiei took the first crawl, and instituted that easy and highly convenient custom. Then, too, the Phascotoherium Bucklandi first told the Archæopteryx Macrura to "lay an egg," and specimens of the first dozen are occasionally met with on the tables of New Haven landladies.

V. The Age of Man is divided by geology into three periods :

(a) The Glacial Period.
(b) Champagne Period.
(c) Later Period.

The first two are times of enjoyable excitement; but after iced champagne in any great quantity, the later period is apt to be rather misty and uncertain.

EXTRACT FROM A NOVEL ON YALE LIFE. •

NOW IN THE PUBLISHER'S HANDS.

THE light was burning dimly in the room of Tom Southerland, the Senior, throwing a shimmering radiance over the luxurious apartment. Shadows played in and out among the recesses and formed weird figures on the armor and with the costly bric-a-brac with which the walls were covered. Luxurious furniture of every description stood around the room in artistic confusion, while the floor was covered with the skins of bears and lions. The heavy silken curtains which covered the doorway to his private boudoir were slightly drawn back, disclosing an apartment also fitted up with the most elegant appointments.

Everything gave evidence to the taste and wealth of their owner.

But, hark! A hurried step is heard, the door opens hastily, and Tom himself enters.

One can see that he is greatly agitated, his hand trembles, his teeth are set, his face is pale! Pouring out a stein of the choicest Amontillado from a cut glass decanter, he tosses it off at a draught, throws himself on one of the divans and buries his face in his hands, "Lost! Lost!" he murmurs with a groan. "Curse him to rob me of my all! Why did I ever play with him? But it's too late now, too late!" What dreadful catastrophe had happened to the possessor of all this magnificence?

Ah, the dreadful demon of gambling! Tom Southerland had lost his last peg top to Bill Spinner in a game for "keeps!"

A SONG.

I MET a little country maid
  One summer, in vacation;—
A pretty, merry, little jade
  Who liked a short flirtation:
"O maiden fair, with blushes rare,
  Your cheeks betray your heart :
You on them Harvard colors wear;
  I fear me, we must part."
    "O Harry, stay,
    I humbly pray,
And look into my eye !"
    Now, that was true
    To Yale: t'was blue;—
Besides, she 'gan to cry.
In heaven's name, what could I do
  But beg her not to sigh?
"You know," she sobbed, when e'er you say,
  I am to Harvard true,
It from my cheeks drives *red* away,
  And makes me, O, so *blue !*"
Now, what, in truth, was I to do,
  But humbly bend my head,
And traitor prove unto the *blue*
  By kissing lips so *red !*

POSITIVELY THE WORST, YET.

Jackson : Now you have her photograph, there's no need of looking so glum.

Jillson : I'm glum because I know it's only a miss—representation.

The sunset's crimson glow has fled,
The cleared firmament o'er head
Is set with stars. The city realms
Are silent as the ancient elms.
The full moon sheds a lustrous hue,
While a brass-buttoned cop, in coat of blue
Paces the campus walks.

Hist, there's a ray from a beacon light!
Hark, 'tis the roar of a bonfire bright!
Merrily leap the flames in glee,
Lighting the front of full Durfee,
Illuminating Farnam and some
Old North,
As th' "arm of the law,"
with his legs set forth,
Determined to quench
that fire

Alas for the man who is swinging his club!
The fire is soon reached, where with one eye there is blood,
There is some one prepared in whose eye there is blood.
He lets fly a tin box, as if loaded with brick,
'Tis the right time for action—the string is now
pulled, the cork in the arms of the sky-god
And the corn is hurled with numberless
to battle with numberless
fires.
S. K.

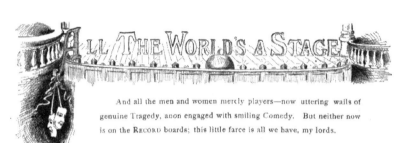

And all the men and women merely players—now uttering wails of genuine Tragedy, anon engaged with smiling Comedy. But neither now is on the RECORD boards; this little farce is all we have, my lords.

THE MEN OF THE PLAY (there are no women)
are :

JOHN YOUNG, ...   The Father of a Son
and
JOHN YOUNGER, ...   The Son of the above mentioned father, and a young man of parts
whom you must know.

They dwell together in the old ancestral cottage which has a garret where the scene is principally laid.

SCENE I.

Library (of course). Son discovered smoking.   Enter Father who has just
finished his last cigar.

Father—John, John, my boy,
    This life's too short for you to waste it thus
    In wreaths of smoke. Come, come, my boy,
    Cast off this foolish costly habit.
Son—Nay, father dear, for twenty years I've tried
    To free me from its grasp, but all in vain.
    I've striven against it, fought it like a dog;
    A hundred times I've almost broke the chain,
    But never quite.
    Each time my hand, my will's executor,
    Has hurled my pipe far, far beyond my ken.
    But e'er the bowl could lose its ruddy glow,
    My panting nostrils sought it out again.
    Ah, father, Nature gives us our desires,
    We're smokers, too, if smokers be our sires.

Father—How! say you then that I am aught to blame
    For your misdeeds ? Well, let it pass.
    And yet methinks the times are surly grown
    When youth presumes to chide the fringeless pate.
Son—Ill words, ill will, and all their ilk be done;
    I'll swear to leave the weed for aye unsmoked
    If you my sire will take the self-same pledge.
Father—Why—son er-yes of course I thus intended,
    (Confound the boy, so shrewd, perverse, provoking,)
    I give you leave to count the bargain ended
    If ere again you find your sire a smoking.
Son—The bargain's done and will to duty bows,
    Naught now remains but to complete our vows.

By the ashes of past pleasure,
Pleasure which I now forget,
By the pipe my chiefest treasure,
By the deadly cigarette,
Solemnly I swear to sever
All connection now and ever
   With the fragrant wreathing smoke,
   Hear, ye things which I invoke.

SCENE II.

In the dimmest part of a very dim attic well supplied with all manner of useless articles, discover a shadowy form crouching behind an old cradle, enveloped in a faintly odorous haze of blue.

Shadowy Form—Smile, smile again, dear heart.
  Since erst this cradle held me as a babe,
  I've not enjoyed such ecstacy divine;
  Long may she burn, sweet-scented Nicotine!
      (*Shadowy form of son discovered stealthily
          stealing up the stairs.*)

Son—Hard have I struggled, and the victory's won,
  But not by me.   The pains which I've endured
  This sen'night now will surely drive me mad
  Unless I ease them with a pipe or two.

Here with my back against this ancient chest
I'll draw sweet solace from my fragrant tube.
But hold! what glowest yonder like a star?
Methinks I see the gleam of a cigar.
Be brave yet cautious.   Useless 'twere to loiter,
I guess I'll steal across and reconnoitre.
   (*Son steals across the open attic and mutters
      to himself as he steals*)—
The poor, good man succumbed.   How sweet he
    looks
Encradled there in clouds of wreathing smoke;

Its fragrance fills the hot and stuffy air.
Suppose I'll have to scare him, well —"Ah, there!"
      (*The result was just what you would
          expect.*)

Father—Young man,
Though I can scarce condone your breach of
    faith,
Yet must I thee forgive when I must crave.
One sluggish week has passed, a baleful week,
Since we conspired to kill each other's joy;

But since these self-same joys our masters prove
And we are servants powerless to revolt,
Let's yield them service and obedient love
And from the door of pleasure draw the bolt.

POOR LITTLE ROSE.

POOR little withered rose!
  'Twas but an hour since
You rested on my lady's breast;
  And all your rosy tints
Blushed, warm with love, the hour you blessed
  And gave my lady all your heart's
    Perfume, poor little rose.

Poor little faded rose!
  I found you on the street:
Your tender petals—once so red—
  Were bruised, as though the feet
Of some one had, with cruel tread,
  Their fragrance crushed. Say was it this
    O rose, poor little rose?

You tell me, little rose,
  That 'twas no cruel tread
That from your heart the perfume crushed,
  And made you hang your head:—
You whisper, and your tone is hushed:
  " I die because *she* cast me off!"
    Alas, poor little rose!

SO TO SPEAK.

SO you have really come to college, have you, Reginald? Well, dear boy, leave your books a few minutes and gather around our editorial knees and listen to the silver-tongued flow of our patriarchal, grey-haired counsel. As we sat, the other evening, chatting over our Kant and coffee with the President, he suddenly clapped us on the back and exclaimed, " Nibbsy, old boy, can you realize it? '89 has really entered! Nice, clean class, '89. Now there's Reginald—fine boy, so to speak. Has a very ingenous countenance, too, as I noticed the other morning, as he was helping out the seniors with their bow. But he's just a trifle, as you might say, fresh—a little verdant, if we may use the expression. Now, old chappie, couldn't you just give him a few tips—put him on to a few points, as it were, which will help him out a little ?"

"That's just what the *Courant* is here for," we responded. And that is how, Reginald, you come to have the benefit of the mellifluous flow of our advice.

Now, Reggy, we all recognize that, it requires considerable ability to enter Yale College, but there have been quite a number of boys before you who managed to get in; and a good many who had less conditions than you had, too. Then there have been a good many who got in but didn't stay long, for some reason or other, either on account of want of proper appreciation of their peculiar merits by the Faculty, or on account of something else. So, my dear boy, that

fifty-thousand-dollar-buy-out-the-college air has an element of superfluousness about it, don't you know ? And, besides, although your pa is the most successful store-keeper at Spruce Corners, the college doesn't care to sell out, just at present, at any rate. If you are looking for a nice, clean, gent's college, there are a number of them lying around loose over the country, which you could get first-class sixty-days' terms on, delivered to any address, express prepaid. But Yale isn't one of that kind. To be sure we didn't win the boat race last June, and rather slipped up on the base-ball championship, and of course we all appreciate your condescension in coming to Yale in face of these facts, but really, Reggy, the college could possibly have gotten on without you.

Another thing we wished to speak to you about is, that cheer of yours. It is a nice cheer, you know, and all that, but really, hadn't you better stick to the old Yale cheer after all ? Your cheer, we imagine, would look in print something like this, Reginald :

" ₁ᵃH—*R*ᴬh raHᴿ—a | H—rah, ʳᵃʰ Rᴬ ᵀ. rah rah Rahᵃ—ᵃ,|. Eighty-Nine—Nine!"

Just a trifle unique, you see. Nine rahs are generally preferred to ten or eight, and it is usual to shout them in unison, you know, although chopping the cheer up in parts, like an anthem sung by a church quartette, no doubt has its advantages. But, of course, if you prefer your style of cheer, the college will at once adopt it, and will have it phonographed and published in prominent papers that the public may recognize it at ball games.

Now, when you have your cheer all nicely settled, Reginald, my boy, and the newness is somewhat worn from the pleasure of carving your class numerals all over the tablets in your recitation rooms, stamping them on your books and hat and everything else you possess, and even the joy of dreaming of what havoc you, a Yale student! will make in the fair hearts up home when the Christmas vacation comes, has become a little stale, you will begin to study hard for the valedictory. Quite proper, my boy, quite proper. That is what "the folks" expect of you. But you won't seem to study much you know. Oh, no! You will spend four solid hours on your Livy, and then rush into Chapel next morning and say to the boy next to you, "Gad! we do have Livy this morning, don't we ?" Then, when you make a cold rush, you think that Smith will tell all the fellows what an awfully bright boy that Reginald is, any way. Now, Reggy, we wouldn't do that if we were you. It's getting to be a pretty old gag by this time, you know—that racket was sprung for the first time in Yale College at Saybrook, A. D. 1701. Do we think you ought to try for valedictory ? Why, yes, of course, my boy; it may be the means of keeping you in your class. Yes, we

THE LADY OR THE TIGER?

know you were valedictorian at Haighseed Academy, and all that,—we exchange with your county paper and read all about it, but you can't depend too much on that, you know. Why, my dear Reginald, every man in the class, to which we have the honor of belonging, was either valedictorian or salutatorian in some first–class–fit–you–for–any–college–in–the–land preparatory school except ourself, and we ought to have been, but as things stand now, the probabilities are that only one of us will be valedictorian here, and he wouldn't consent to take the position but for keeping up the reputation of the class. A class really ought to have a valedictorian, you know.

But you will get over dreaming about high stand in about seven months and a half; then the object of your ambition will be a *Lit.* editorship. That's right, Reginald; quite in form, doncher-know, me deah boy, as they say at, aw, Columbia. You won't be elected—you don't write very good graveyard poetry, you know—but then you had better try. It has been a great satisfaction to us to speak of "when we were writing for the *Lit.*"

Now, Reggy, we will close our fatherly talk with you with a few simple instructions which we wish some one had given us when we were a freshman. Don't laugh at the choir: it means well, and can probably sing as well as you can. Always say "Chestnuts" at an instructors's class-room joke, whether it is a brand-new juicy one or not. That is the proper act. Always treat subscription men as low-lived villians trying to defraud you. This is for their sake, as if you didn't do it the surprise might be too much for their nerves.

Now, Reggy, my boy, run out and play!

THE OLD CURIOSITY SHOP.

"AND who is this, sir?" I asked of the keeper who was conducting me, the oldest living graduate, through the corridors of the building which, in my younger days, was known as the *Old Lab.*, but now bears the more dignified and suggestive name of Asylum for College Cranks and Curiosities.

The being in the cell to which I pointed was a jolly-faced man whose fat sides were encased in a suit which showed little of the original material through the thick stains of paint and paste which covered it. The cell was crowded with tools of all kinds; here were saws and ropes, rakes and hoes, paste and paint pots, shears and brushes, and a lawn mower marked Y. C. The inmate was trying to select the homeliest from three styles of authorized wall-paper, which he proceeded to hang on the walls with the pattern inverted. The flakes that peeled off his suit here and there disclosed the many colored paints which under various regimes had been authorized by the Faculty for college rooms. "This subject," said my guide, "was for many years a man of affairs on the campus. He was the college painter, paper-hanger, leaf-raker, tree-trimmer, path-straightener, cleaner up of bon-fires, and substitute or janitor. He served long to the best of his ability, and

finally went mad on discovering that he had done something without a mistake." Just then we heard a terrible kicking against a cell door which was of boiler-plate. A glance through a bullseye showed a fierce figure clad in garments in which blood and mud strove for superiority of color. "A foot-ball player at play," whispered my trembling attendant who I afterward heard had once been on the Harvard eleven, and he dragged me away from the sound of those copper-toed kicks, which were now being led with cries of "Jump on that Harvard man; he's your meat."

I was next shown a number of inoffensive looking young men seated about a mammoth waste-basket. This receptacle was divided into compartments, each labelled with a name like News, Lit., etc. Into the compartments these representatives of the college press threw scraps of scribbled paper. Now and then one more erratic than the rest would throw in a fire-brand which would set its neighbors ablaze, but after a little fuming all would go on as monotonously as before. Hung about the apartments were cheap prints of the new Y. M. C. A. Building, and the cruzade to Beers', towards which the inmates looked at intervals for inspiration. I could easily see that these men were editors whom over-work had driven to distraction.

BEFORE.

I saw no sadder sight in all my wanderings. One apartment bore above its door the inscription, "Another fellow's room." Tnere were two young men here—one with an air of intelligence which the other very plainly lacked. The former sat at a desk in the attitude of study. I noticed on closer observatiou that his form trembled at intervals with rage, which was only restrained by the chains which bound him to his seat. Nor had I far to look for the cause of these paroxysms. The second young man had evidently just dropped into "Another fellow's room," and was running on after this style: "What do you think of the eleven this term. Psychology is a grind, isn't it? Got any cigarettes? Give me a match. Blank 'ill get on the crew; don't you think so?" I thought the studious man would break his manacles; so I left him and his tormentor. I had no need to ask my guide for the interpretation of this scene. Even when I was in college such characters as these were frequent. I was now hurried past several open but narrow rooms, each containing a single occupant. I caught glimpses of a man trying on a purple spangled vest. Five other vests of striking design hung on chairs and bed-posts, and there were racks for neckties on three sides of the rooms; by a judicious arrangement of mirrors the gentleman was enabled to detect and eradicate any wrinkle which might appear to mar the perfect fit of his apparel. In his delirious chatterings I could detect the meaningless words "crushed strawberry," and "canary bird food." As my conductor remarked, this patient was a perfectly harmless example of mingled crank and curiosity. In another of these narrow cells was a man who continually marched with military tread in his allotted space, while his hands moved as though in the act of beating a drum. "Woolsey Battalion Drum Corps" was posted over the one window, and as we lost sound of the footfalls, my attendant said, "Drum did it," and smiled a ghastly smiie. Still again my gaze rested upon what they told me was a track athlete. The cinders from his little grate fire had been carefully packed down at one end of the room; the one chair was marked "Grand Stand, 15 cents extra," and upon that little cinder track the poor fellow was going through the motions of a sprint-runner. What little space remained was filled with dumb-bells, clubs, and jumping apparatus.

You will scarcely believe me when I tell you that room was found in the Old Lab. for so large a collection, and in truth the inmates were sometimes crowded. Here was the senior who had tried four times for the Glee Club, and though four times weighed in the scales, yet was found wanting, and gravitated to the choir and thence to the curiosity shop, and here the tennis fiend, with his eternal invitations to come out and have a set before recitation; and the would-be humorist driving his associates to deeper levels of despair by his ill-timed jest and pre-Noachian pun.

Being the oldest living graduate, the explorations had tired me much, and moreover I was overwhelmed by the memories of my earlier days which these sights had aroused within me. I therefore prepared to leave

AFTER.

the building, and as I bid farewell to the keeper from the doorstep, I saw a man within, standing with his back to the window and looking out. The strange reversal of his head attracted my attention to its idiotic leer. "Who may that be?" I asked. "That," said the keeper, as he turned to go, "is the man who stares at the rear gallery in chapel."

NO ROSE WITHOUT ITS THORN.

Do you know, of earthly blisses,
    None are half so sweet as kisses,
        Pretty Miss!
And, your lips, than other misses',
        I would kiss.

Then the village maid looked shyly,
Whilst I kissed her—Curse all wily
        Maids!—in brief:
She had held a needle, slyly,
        'Twixt her teeth!

AT LAST!

Not long ago a knock was heard at the door of a freshman.

"Come in!"

A dapper young man, with a suspicious looking book, entered.

"I came to see if——"

"Oh, yes! You came to see if you could get my subscription to the class nine. I might have known you were a classmate of mine. You have the same fresh look about you that——"

"Sir! I came to see if I could get——"

"Oh! you are on the *Gospel Union News*, hey? Well, now, when I come to look at you squarely in the face, I do see some signs of a dyspeptic Christian about you, You all have that quiet, unsophisticated——"

"Sir! This is an outrage! I came to get your——"

"Oh! I beg your pardon. I should have seen it before. You came to get me to subscribe for the football team. Dear me! How wise those foot-ball men are. They don't come around themselves, but send

THEY THINK THEY HAVE PUT THE NEW RECITATION HALL IN THE RIGHT PLACE;
BUT HAVE THEY?

"NIGGER BABY" IN ANCIENT ROME. HITHERTO SUPPOSED TO BE THE STONING OF
STEPHEN THE MARTYR.

some one who looks as if he'd never seen a foot-
ball——"

"Sir! Sir! I came to get your sub——"

"Yes! yes! Of course you did—for the University
crew. It's my duty, you know, as a freshman, of
course, and I——"

"Sir! I am not here to be fooled with. I came to
get——"

"Oh! you are on the Junior Promenade committee.
Well, now! who would ever have thought *you* guilty
of dancing. Why, you look as if a breath would blow
you away."

"See here, young man. Will or will you not——"

"Subscribe to the *Lit.*? Dear me, are you a *Lit.*
editor? Ye gods! It is so. I see the divine light in
your eyes. The dignity that shows itself in thy every
movement hath made thee known! Yes. Oh, young
man! I know it is the *Lit.* that you wish me to take,
but I don't want it. I also know it is the *Yale Literary Magazine!* I also know it is the oldest college
periodical in America. From my earliest days I have
heard of it. From the Atlantic to the Pacific its praises
are sounded, but honestly, young man. I——"

"But I am *not* a *Lit.* editor. I came to see if I
could get your subscription——"

"To the Lacrosse team? Well, now, that is your
place. I might have known it. You must make a
good player! You are such a thin, cadaverous-looking
youth; your arms are long, your legs are marvels,
your eyes are sharp——"

But the visitor was gone and the freshman was
alone. He smiled a little and said, "I don't think any
more of his tribe will call on *me*." And he was right.

RECITATION IN MAY.

THE bell strikes eight, then two; the hum subsides;
  Across the room the tardy straggler strides
And throws himself, by gravity drawn down,
Upon the bench despite the tutor's frown.
The roll-call now begins, the "Here," and "Here,"
In tones from bass to treble greet the ear,
While now one man with voice unlike the rest,
Cries "Present" (smiles of class are unsupprest).
With text-book, marking-book, and pencil too,
The tutor next attempts to flunk a few,
One fellow rises, guesses hard and long,
Is prompted some but finally guesses wrong;
Another man is called, a book is closed,
It drops upon the floor—that fraud's exposed.
A third essays the task, is fortunate
Enough to rush, he takes his seat elate;
The class applauds, confusion reigns supreme,
The noise disturbs some sleeping student's dream,
He wakes. The uproar once begun will last
Until the recitation hour is past.
Sometimes the air is thick with paper wads,
And tooth-picks fly across the room in squads.
Again two fellows on the hindmost seat
Begin a lively "scrap" with hands and feet.
The hour drags slowly by, it seems a day
Since it began. The merry month of May
Is far more suitable for play than work,
For boys pursue the one, the other shirk,
They hear the tutor's "that 'll do" no more.
A rush, the recitation hour is o'er.

THE CHESTNUT.

PHYSIOLOGICALLY AND PSYCHOLOGICALLY CON-
SIDERED—ITS RELATIONS TO MORAL PHE-
NOMENA.

Difficulty of defining it.

§ 1. To attempt at the beginning of the investigation the definition of a subject whose subtleties neces-
sitate for their comprehension careful analytical and
synthetical processes as well as a rigid scrutiny of
ethical relations and argumentative refu-
tations of those popular misconceptions
which militate against the testimony of
consciousness is manifestly unsatisfactory. For this
reason we can at the beginning only "define the scope
of our inquiries"—J. Stuart Mill: *Logic*, Introductory,
§ 1.

What is a chestnut?

§ 2. The subject matter of our investigation is the
chestnut. *But what is a chestnut?* We
reply without hesitation and in direct opposition to antagonistic theories that a
chestnut is a chestnut. But it may be urged on the
Objection. other hand in accordance with the posi-
tivist theory that nothing is done before
it is done, that before we can take this ground we must
first prove that there is such a thing as a chestnut; in
other words that there exists a material entity which
when it confronts a sentient soul, so to speak, arouses
in that soul the consciousness of chestnutness.

§ 3. What then are our proofs? To this inquiry
we reply in general:

(1) Generally recognized.

(1) No human being with moderately developed
powers of reflection ever existed who
could not recognize a chestnut when it
was brought within his range of vision.

(2) No nation or community of human beings, how-
(2) Vocabu- lary found in all languages. ever degraded, has ever been found
whose vocabulary does not contain some
terms to express the idea of chestnut and
its attendant relations to external spread-
outness.

Two-fold division.

§ 4. The chestnut admits of a two-fold division—
into the *physiological* and *psychological.*
The one distinguishes and defines the
capacities for good and evil exercised on
man, in what may be called his physical capacity, by
the material concrete chestnut, and the other classifies
and arranges the emotions brought into exercise by the
quasi ideal or abstract chestnut as affecting the sentient
soul.

Is the chest- nut a cate- gory?

§ 5. Many able thinkers hold that the chestnut is a
category, that it is simple, original and
indefinable, that it precedes *a priori* in
point of time whatever follows it. While
we are not prepared to deny as it were
the validity of this theory, we reply provisionally that
No. the chestnut is not a category; that in so
far as it is capable of analysis it may be
analyzed into elements of a still more elementary character.

Sedlitz is perhaps hypercritical in his discussion of
this point when he says: "Those who hold that the
Testimony of Sedlitz. chestnut is a category entirely lose sight
of the Aristotelian and Kantian doctrines
and are even so unphilosophical as to ig-
nore *in toto* one of the fundamental axioms of all
science,—"*de gustibus non disputandum sed amor
omnia vincit.*"—*Essays on Anthropomorphism* LVII.
Chap. CCL., §§ 48, 49.

Mill is equally clear and forcible when he says:

SOME TENNIS EXPRESSIONS.

A VOLLEY.　　A FOUR-HANDED SERVE.　A DRIVE TO THE BASE LINE.　　A SMASH.

J. Stuart Mill. "Nothing can be more illogical than the argument of the categorical school of philosophers. They take a premise, the absolute truth of which is far from certain—namely, that the first chestnuts were those which the monkey obtained from the red-hot stove through the involuntary agency of a cat's paw, used as a cat's paw, and on this flimsy groundwork they found the entire tottering edifice of their theory."—*Lectures on Inductive Logic,* Chap. XIV, § 29. See also for an interesting discussion illustrating this subject.—*The Forty Years Correspondence between Presidents McCosh and Elliott on Professionalism in College Athletics. Letters* Nos. 2024-8, For concrete examples of chestnuts see the *Yale Log*—e. g. "COURANT out to-morrow," etc.

§ 6. The chestnut in both its physical and psychical capacities is more or less the object of desire. Why this desire forms a part of man's moral nature we cannot say—we simply know from the testimony of consciousness that it exists and influences our outward action.

The chestnut an object of desire.

Moreover we are conscious that this desire has not been acquired, but has always been as it were latent in our natures. As soon as the infant awakens to rememberable consciousness he finds himself in possession of a desire for chestnuts. According to Dugald Stewart—"The object of hunger is not happiness but food "—(*Active and Moral Powers,* book 1, Chap. 1,) thus the object of the infant's desire for chestnuts is chestnuts and not the pleasure which the gratification of the desire gives.

Desire for chestnuts acquired at an early age.

When the mother sees her child indulge his desire for chestnuts to an extent dangerous to the orderly development of the other sensibilities she invariably endeavors to stimulate his moral introspectiveness by asking, "can you not see by looking inward upon your moral nature and by awakening into progressive activity your ethical self-consciousness that a self-sacrificing self-denial of the gratification of slavish appetite is a more ennobling impulse than selfish obedience to the same; is not an "abstract chestnut in the breast " a higher object of desire than a concrete chestnut in the stomach?" To these searching inquiries the child can give but one answer—"Chestnuts !"

Experiences of childhood.

§ 7. That the chestnut, whether abstract or concrete, is uniformly pleasant or painful, usually more the latter than the former, is the testimony of the ablest metaphysicisis.

Butler proposes the following scheme— When the monopolists has chestnuts and the poor workingman has none, how can you wonder at crime?—(*Laws of Love,* Chap. XXV, §§ 27 and 28.)

Benjamin Butler.

Onegegan urges—"Ould Ireland's the place where the shamrock grows Ameriky's flower 's the chistnut—(*Celtic Lyrics.*)

Ony Onegegan.

Longfellow also asserts "Beneath the spreading chestnut tree the village smithy stands."

Henry W. Longfellow.

On the same subject Von Tannenbaum says,--" It does not with the Utilitarians and Hedonists find the moral norm of

Herr Von Tannenbaum.

Crosseye (rather near-sighted): " Know where your sister is, Jack? I have this dance with her, and I can't find her anywhere."

    Jack: "Well. you're on the right trail, anyway ; follow it up."

the subject-object in contradistinction to the antagonistic object-object theories of those who otherwise hold differently." Cf, also Fliegende Blatter.

Pursuing the same line of thought the *Record* says—

Yale Record. "The Italians live mostly on chestnuts," also "What is the matter with calling dropped men chestnuts?"

Darwin. Darwin adds "There are thirty-four different varieties of chestnuts.—*Origin of Species*, LV, Chap. XXI, § 12."

OBJECTIONS, COUNTER-OBJECTIONS AND CROSS COUNTER OBJECTIONS.

The theories cited above are all open to the same objections,—they are incomplete, they are incorrect and their meaning is often obscured by superabundant rhetoric.

In opposition to the above cited authorities we hold that the chestnut is not a category, that it is more or

Our Theory. less the object of desire, that the desire is weakened by repetition, especially in the case of the bodily appetite, that in both the abstract and the concrete its relations are such as may be mastered by an infant; and finally that our

No insects on it. theory is the only one which a rightly developed intellect can adopt as a norm or standard, so to speak, of reflection and external action.

ON THE HEIGHTS.

Beyond the seething, boiling tide
The city lies spread out. The roar
Of truckteams sweetly sounds afar.
The Jersey flats lie seaward spread,
While near at hand the pastoral goat
Meanders aimlessly. And at
Our feet Hoboken slumbers on
In dreamy, dusty, beery sleep.
Jersey City, 1884.

JOHN SULLIVAN MILL.

THIS is eminently a transcendental age. While Herbert Spencer and his school are thundering against the portals of that strong castle, conservative Philosophy, while from the dark and threatening clouds of anarchy the lightning of approaching iconoclasm flashes with a lurid light, while the realism of the present is succumbing to the fast advancing squadrons panoplied with all the glittering effulgence of a chivalrous Charlemagne of romance, while the gilded salons, turreted chateaux, exquisite courtiers of the *Ancient Régime* have been remanded to the limbo of roseate sentimentality,

"That bourne from which no traveller returns,"

while the troops of mighty Britain are meeting in the fatal field of Mars, the murderous myriads of the cultry Soudan, while the skies look down in mute horror, and the earth, mother of Isis

---

A GLIMPSE OF YALE JOURNALISM.

Below we offer a page from each of the Yale papers. Our object is merely to embody in a material form the popular conceptions of the characteristic foibles of each. Here are the papers in the order of their founding.

AN : ASPIRACION,

Alle : lyfe : ys : bvtte : a : cloude
  of : smoake :
Alle : else : ys : bvtte : a : pass-
  ynge : joake :
Maie : Hee : be : hang'd : y't
  stoppes : to : croke :
I : quaffe : my : glasse : and
  sitte : and : smoake.

A NEEDLESS ALARM.

Mr. S— was spending the winter at W—, being impecunious as well as a marked man, that was all he had to spend. Going down street one afternoon with his friend Tom B—, he suddenly stopped and grasped his arm. "Do you see that ?"

"What ?" said Tom excitedly, " that beautiful maiden with an aureole of blonde hair like a—like a——"

"Oh, no, no, oh the devil, no."

"Wh—wh, wh-a-at, is it then ?"

"That—there—oh, Holy Moses and the chariot of fire—that—there!"

"Which ? what ? where ? Are you drunk or only crazy ?"

"That—that long-haired —his vest doesn't make connections, his—"

"See here," interrupted the other sardonically, "are you often taken so, or—"

"No, no, look, oh, John Rogers, and his fourteen twins! Right there!"

"Oh, that—that is nothing but a stray freshman, who happens to be a dig."

"Oh,—h," said the other, breathing a sigh of relief, and they both passed into the afternoon shadows, while the unconscious freshman ambled back to town.

ICH HUGGTE SIE.

We sat as close as close could be;
  I asked her, if I might,
She acquiesced, and so you see
  Right there I hugged her tight.

'Twas on the sofa that we sat—
  The lamp was turned down low,
And she was so attractive that
  I hugged her tight, you know.

ENNUI.

The embers dead to me proclaim
The weariness of life. The fire
Is out ; the ashes, cold and gray,
Are sleeping gracefully ;—to me
No rest has come, no rest can
  come,
Till I, too, like the fire, get up
and go.

TERRIBLE TREATMENT.

It was a dark night as I rode along in a miserable caboose attached to a slow freight train. The train hands sat about in various attitudes of repose, occasionally making a contribution to the sawdust box in front of the stove. At length we stopped, and imagine my delight when a fresh young maiden entered the caboose. After a little skillful manœuvering I entered into conversation with the young lady, and was soon telling her some of my thrilling adventures. By this time the train hands had left the car and were distributed along the train. Gradually waxing facetious, I remarked to the young lady that I would ring for a lunch, and then pulled the bell rope. I had to walk twenty miles to the next station.

MABETTE.

In faith it is an old-world name,
  Mabette,
But though mankind should give
  you game,
My soul with love shall ever
  flame, Mabette,
E'en though these verses be but
  lame, Mabette,
I love you, sweet one, all the
  same, Mabette, Mabette.

At a recent service in the Chapel of Bidhaeg University, the Rev. Mr. Spouter preached a 60 min. sermon in 15 min. 3 sec. Mr. Spouter now holds the ecclesiastical belt.

YALE LOG.

Smith '89 is ill.
Chapel to-morrow at 8.10
Longhair '87 has an article in the current G.U.N.
The highest building in the worlk is the Washington Monument.
It may not be generally known that eur president was valedictorian of the class of 1847.
A bald-headed man on being told his hairs were said to have made $25,000 out of his professiou.
Sullivan, the puolist is numbered, said he would like some back numbers.
A numerous petition has been offered to the Harvard faculty for voluntary prayers.
Between five and six hundred men attend chapel exercises.
The fire insurance companies in Hartford have a total capital of 17,000,000,-000.
Prof. Beaiyl gave some interesting selections at his readings last evening the most favoritist piece was: "The Curlew shall not sing to-night."
Prof. Jeremiah Hegenbotham of Bidhaeg University has just published a new work on Ethics which is spoken of very highly.

The following list will show the relative standing of the different clubs of the Connecticut State Cock-fighting association:

	LOST.	WON.
Mt. Carmel,	5	2
Ansonia.	4	3
New Haven,	3	3
Bridgeport,	2	4

Mr. John Scudder of Oberlin, O., has succeed in walking a mile and three laps cp hill on roller skates in 5 min. and 3 sec. against a strong wind.

Be sure and try Dyees' Cayenne & Cubed Cough Candy. Every student should have it. Freshmen cry for it. Cures everything.

Tutoring by a recent undergraduate. Harper's text used. Refers to students at Milford and Cheshire. Never skipt long words. Call and examine.

A new line of checked suitings, different pattern in every square. Plan of Philadelphia, showing all public buildings, is the favorite suiting. Guff & Co.

To Rent. A very desirable room. Fourth story, skylight. Cornet playing next door. Terms reasonable. Apply to the college inspector.

LETTER FROM AMERICAN SCHOOL AT ATHENS.

WE are filled with enthusiasm over athletics here. Among the attractions of the *Greek National Exhibition*, set for 1887, there will be an exact reproduction of the *Olympic Games*, and, if successful, they will be continued every four years. Since the discontinuance of these games a few years ago—[In the Memorabilia of the *Lit.* we find August, 967 B. C., as the date of the last meet. Ed.]—track athletics have fallen somewhat into stagnation ; but their revival will undoubtedly rouse up the great interest once taken in them. Our prospects never were brighter. Thirteen candidates have appeared for the palm-leaf prize in the 440 Stadia run. Of these the most promising is Xenophon, who is said to have made it in one hemera. Œdipus Tyrannus, the crack sprinter from Corinth, is his most dangerous competitor. For the 10 parassang dash, six candidates have appeared thus far, of whom Enteuthen Exelauni will probably make the hardest fight for it. He ran in the Persian games a few years ago, lowering the Babylonian record. On putting the hoplon there is but one candidate, " Ho " Barbaros, who can put it five days' journey with a little practice. Digamma, who holds the inter-collegiate championship in digging Greek roots, will not enter this year on account of poor health. Basileus, the captain of our team, will ride in the chariot race, and will also contend against Charon, the stroke of the Styx crew, in the single-sculling match on the straight-way course between the town and Poluspuloisboro Thalasses— (our Exchange editor has been unable to find this place on the map, but it is probably near Olympia. Ed.) Palm leaves will be the prizes for most of the events, but the winner of the boxing match with the ox-hide cestus will be crowned with laurel and preceded up Broadway, Athens, by the Hellenic Brass Band from Hellertown. The gods have kindly consented to referee the games and Venus will award the prizes. Many coaches and other vehicles have been chartered for the occasion, among them a tally-ho by Aristophanes (Medic), and the Bricks of the Kai Gar Omega fraternity, Season tickets for the games can now be obtained at the Contemplatory of the School. Single admission is 10 oboli.   SOCRATES.

Mr. Oarsman (on the crew): Have you seen the Yale tank ?
Miss Pharmington (innocently): No, I haven't met him.

Atte Chrismastyde yᵉ merrie wyghte
Flyes o'er ye snow to tune of belles
Yᵗ sownde acrosse yᵉ frostie nighte,
And wake yᵉ sylente frozen delles
Yᵗ sleepe see fayre and whyte.

Vponne yᵉ ice in colours brighte
Yᵉ skaters are a merrie syghte
Atte Christmas-tyde.

Yᵉ craeklinɡ yvle-loɡɡe blazes bryɡhte,
Yᵉ steamynɡe ale is foamynɡe whyte,
With mistle-toe yᵉ walles are diɡhte.
Whenne pealynɡe chymes yᵉ mirnɡhte
Yᵉ Christmas waites Yʳᵉ synɡynɡe swell
cheere and sonɡe and fulle delyɡhte
Atte christmas-tyde.

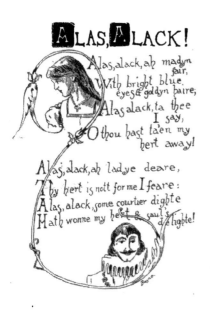

ALAS, ALACK!

Alas, alack, ah madyn fair,
With bright blue.
eyes & goldyn haire;
Alas alack, ta thee
I say,
O thou hast ta'en my
hert away!

Alas, alack, ah ladye deare,
Thy hert is nott for me I feare:
Alas, alack, some courtier dighte
Hath wonne my hert & sau'ls delighte!

A FEARFUL CHARGE. STARTLING REVELATIONS.

THE following letters from the pen of one of our prominent professors, who, heretofore, has enjoyed an enviable reputation, will put him in a position from which it will be difficult for him to escape. However painful it is to us to publish them, we feel constrained, from a sense of duty, to perform the unpleasant task. The letters have been handed to us by Mrs. J. K. Lions, a respectable widow, whose son enters college this fall.

NEW HAVEN, July 2, 1884.
(Private.)   (Confidential.)   (To be burned.)
MRS. J. K. LIONS:
Dear Madam:
 Your letter with reference to your son has been received. I may state that through my instrumentality he passed without conditions, thus winning the $100 prize which you mentioned as being offered by his school. If you think that my services have been of any value, you may express your appreciation as you hinted.
  Yours very respectfully,
    B. F. SINISTER.

NEW HAVEN, July 10, 1884.
(Private.)   (Personal.)   (To be destroyed.)
MRS. J. K. LIONS:
Dear Madam:
 Check for fifty dollars (50) received.
(To be burned.)   B. F. SINISTER.

OUTRAGEOUS CHARGES.

THE fearful charges made against Prof. Sinister in the last *Record* only show to what desperate straits the calumniators of that gentleman are forced. It is well-known that this scandal has originated in an intention to injure the Professor's candidacy as nominee for Alderman in the Eighth Ward. We are authorized to publish the following letters:

HOLLYTOWN, CT., June 3, '84.
Prof. B. F. Sinister:
 REVEREND AND HONORED MENTOR—I have a son, the very image of his dear departed father, who intends entering your institution this year. Inasmuch as my aunt had a second cousin who married a half brother of your wife's first husband, I *know* you will be interested in looking after my Johnny and aiding him in whatever way you can. I see various channels in which I *know* you can be useful to him. His school offers a prize of $100 to the young man passing the best entrance examination.
  Yours, in the bonds of friendship,
    JEMIMA KOSSUTH LIONS.

A day or two after the receipt of this letter Johnny Lions reached New Haven. Prof. Sinister took him in charge and found that as things then stood young Mr. Lions could by no possibility pass the entrance examinations. He immediately took the young man to a private tutor in New Haven who agreed, for the moderate sum of $50, to tutor the young man, *and get him through.* Prof. Sinister then wrote to Mrs. Lions *this* letter, which his slanderers have contemptibly failed to publish. Fortunately he retained a copy of it :

NEW HAVEN, June 7, '84.
Mrs. J. K. Lions:
 DEAR MADAM—Your son received in good order, comparatively fresh. He is so green that he cannot possibly get into college without tutoring. The most reasonable tutor in New Haven is Snobbs, A. B., who guarantees to get your son into college for the moderate sum of $50. Let me know immediately if you accept the terms, and Snobbs will begin his work. Payment after Johnny gets his papers.
  Yours, etc.,   B. F. SINISTER.

Mrs. Lions telegraphed as follows:

Prof. B. F. Sinister, New Haven, Conn.:
I accept; Snobbs a brick.   JEMIMA.
5 collect.

EFFECTS OF JACK AND BOB'S COLLEGE VACATION.

Ethel: No, Alice, I wouldn't have to go you on that matinee this afternoon.
Alice: O, its smooth and its too easy to shake Mr. Cornhill, that tacky heeler of yours.
Ethel: Sure, I believe I'll get a curve and go after all. Say, Alice, I would have to match you for the checks.

With all the pride and impatience of a fond mother Mrs. Lions waited as long as possible and finally wrote *this* letter:

HOLLYTOWN, CT., June 25, 1884.
Prof. Sinister:
DEAR SIR—Isn't the ordeal 'most over for poor Johnny? Let me know please. If he gets through, I shall be so grateful to you for your assistance that I shall send you a barrel of our best crab-apple cider.
Yours, J. K. L.

To this letter Prof. Sinister made the reply quoted in last week's *Record,* and printed as his *first* letter. It is foolish to have to explain that the phrase "*If you think that my services have been of any value, you may express your appreciation as you hinted,*" refers to the barrel of crab-apple cider, a legitimate gift of a grateful widow for a disinterested favor done her by the much slandered professor. Shortly after this the following letter, containing a check for $50, PAYABLE TO FITZWILLIAM SNOBBS, was received by Prof. Sinister:

HOLLYTOWN, CT., July 5, 1884.
DEAR SIR—Accept a lone widow's heartfelt thanks. I enclose check for Mr. Snobbs, not knowing his address. Will ship the cider next week.
Gratefully, MRS. J. K. LIONS.

In reply to this Professor Sinister sent letter No. 2, as printed in the *Record.*

We append the following declaration:

I have read the foregoing, and assert that it is absolutely true, as regards myself, in every detail.
(Signed) FITZWILLIAM SNOBBS.

Prof. Sinister affirms that the words "Personal," "Private," etc., appended to the printed copies of his letters, *are not genuine, but in a counterfeit hand.* We trust this vindication will prove complete and satisfactory.

MELASIPPOS

Words by GILBERT & THOMPSON.   **AN OPERETTA.**   Score by SLADE & SULLIVAN.

DRAMATIS PERSONÆ.

Briareus,................ ....A Schoolmaster	Theseus,.............................
Melasippos, ... ⎫	Hercules,.............................
Orpheus,............... .... ⎬ Scholars of	Boreas, ... ⎬ Scholars.
Castor and Pollux,............. ⎪ Briareus.	Nestor, ...
Ajax,........ .... ⎭	Philomela,...... ....Daughter of Briareus.

OVERTURE (by a full orchestra).

Pianissimo.   Accelerando.   Piano forte.   Con moto.   Fortissimo.   Let-loose.

ACT I.—SCENE I.

PROLOGUE.

In Berkshire, not so many years ago,
Dwelt a fair maiden whom my muse shall know
As Philomela, wise Briareus' daughter,
The local pedagogue—and many sought her.

Her father early had conceived the plan,
That Phil. should wed an educated man,
And to that end, one day, addressed the school,
Which sore had felt the pedagogic rule.

SCENE 2.

Briareus :

Ye who adore my Philly from afar,
Who long to have Briareus as pa—
The one of you who shows the purest sand,
Shall have, I swear it, Philomela's hand.

So as the olden heroes sailed from Greece
To win renown and get the golden fleece,
Do you embark to win renown at Yale,
And four years hence return to tell your tale.

CHORUS OF SCHOLARS.

Scherzo.   Crescendo.   Ah there.   Sickatto.   Come againo.   Con busto.

We ac-cept your propo-sition, And we beg with all contri-tion
That you'll par-don us our bold-ness in de-mand-ing

our boldness   in demanding
What the faculty require, And the world at large admire,
A certificate of good and moral standing.

Briareus :

Tho' your qualifications are slender,
And my conscience abnormally tender,
I'll send you the letters by earliest mail;
May the angels deal kindly with me and old Yale.

ACT II.— SCENE I.

[Four years have elapsed.]

Briareus :

Four years their course have sped,
Of my scholars now returned,

That one shall Philomela wed
Who best her heart and hand has earned.

Enter Orpheus.

Briareus :

And what has Orpheus done to win the prize?

Orpheus :

I've sung the old, old songs; *there* honor lies.

(Sings.)   I am on the Glee Club,
'Twas a pretty close rub,
For at least half a dozen sang higher,

But my clothes had the tone
Which my voice didn't own,
And besides I'd a friend on the choir.

You should come to our show,
All the best people go
Where we sing of the " Bold Fisher Lad,"
Where we warble and bray
And shed tears for " P. Gray."
With the audience howling like mad.

Briareus :

'Tis well, 'tis well, you surely ought to win;
But, Theseus, what have your achievements been?

1st Base.   2d Base.   3d Base.   Crescendo.   Struckouto.   Diminuendo.

Most rev - erend sir, Fath - er of her, whom I a - dore,
List to my tale, My a -chieve - ments at Yale, I ask no more.

2. In freshman year
  I handled the sphere,
  On our class nine.
  Team came from Boston,
  Which Harvard lost on,
  Glory part mine.

3. In time of sparcity
  Got on the 'varsity,
  Summit of fame.
  Each man in college,
  Small tho' his knowledge,
  Knew me by name.

4. Games with our foes,
  As every one knows,
  We won by the *score,*
  That is my claim,
  Old Briareus, to fame—
  Hand the maid o'er.

Briareus :

All very well, but you're going too fast;
Before I decide, I must hear from the last.

Nestor :

I am Nestor of the *Lit.* board,
Yale's Sahara publication,
I have long years toiled and striven,
And I now can write a leader,
Deal with the most weighty problems;
Tendencies cannot elude me
I can analyze men's motives,
I live on the dusty top-shelf,
I am down on wit and humor,
I have one conceit archaic,
Every year I sell a phantom,
Ghostly, title to the *Banner,*
Thus have I deserved your daughter,
Give her not unto these others,
I am a mug-wump of the Yaleses,
I'm the envied of the college.

Briareus :

Let Ajax now some worthy reason show,
Why I on him my daughter should bestow.

Ajax [sings; air, Theseus' song]:

A foot-ball rusher am I,
In tricks and manœuvres I'm sly
  I tackle like fun,
  As tho' shot from a gun,
Every fellow who tries to get by.

With Princeton we played in New York,
Their mouths sadly needed a cork;
  They slowly went back,
  Before our attack,
And we soon had a corner in Pork.

As reward for my prowess, I claim,
Your child, Philomela by name;
  She's captured my heart,
  With which I can't part,
So we must be one and the same.

Briareus :

'Tis well, my dear fellow, but which of you wins,
I cannot decide till I hear from the twins.

Castor and Polux:

DUET.　　　*Con expressivo.*　　*Chestnuto.*　　*Going faro.*　　*Only to the caro.*

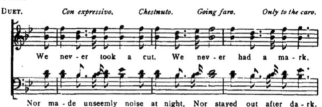

We nev - er took a cut. We nev - er had a ma - rk,

Nor ma - de unseemly noise at night, Nor stayed out after da - rk.

2. We never flunked, we learned
   Our lessons over night,
   We always did the optionals
   And always got them right.

3. We've never been involved
   In tumult or dissension,
   We never slept in sermon time
   But paid the best attention.

4. We're called the model twins,
   We've always been high stand.
   Instructor, counselor, dear friend,
   Give us your daughter's hand.

Briareus:

But you are two—tho' twins, 'tis true,
I'm undecided whether
This one or that should be my son;
I can't take both together.

Castor and Pollux:

We always count for one,
　We can't be told apart,
Two souls with mind enough for one,
Two bodies with one heart.

Briareus:

Steel-lunged, bull-throated Boreas has the floor.

Boreas:

List but a moment and the tale is o'er.

(Sings.)　I have taken all the prizes
　　　Which were offered there at Yale
For chief excellence in speaking;
　　　At my coming rivals quail.

Should you ask me for the *modus*
　Operandi of success,
I can give it in one stanza,
　Try it, you won't make a mess.

For the Junior Exhibition
　You must take a subject trite.
Roman Catholics and Slavery
　(With quotations) win the fight.

If you spread the eagle's pinions,
　Talk of Liberty and guff,
You can capture every honor,
　Only try it long enough.

Briareus:

Well, Hercules, a man of your vast frame
Must have a solid basis for his claim.

Hercules:

I rowed among the winning crew
　In June, you may remember,
And helped to gain the victory, too,
　From Princeton last November.
And this should clearly prove to you
　That Philomela is my due.

Briareus:

Where all have done so well, 'tis hard to say,
Yet Hercules, methinks, has won the—

Melasippos:

　　　　　　　　　　　　　　Stay!

Briareus:

　Great sorrow! must we listen to your bray?

Melasippos:

I gained all my knowledge by skinning and cribbing.
I led the whole college in crawling and fibbing.
　I've twenty excuses for every omission,
　I try different ruses in each new position.

Briareus:

　And do you expect
　I'll deign to select
　A suitor, whose claim is so feeble—

Melasippos:

Well, no, but the fact is,
I put into practice
My own rule of action, and, well,
　To be in good season,
　Without any reason,
I yesterday wed Philomel.　　　　[*Exit.*

Briareus:

Alas, alas! for my beautiful plan,
Philomela elopes with a good for naught man.

Chorus of disappointed lovers:

He stole a march, ah, wretched theft—
We did the work, and we got left.

Briareus:

The wretch, the villain! by desert,
We'd capture him and slay him,
But since he's skinned his way through life,
It's only fair to flay him.

GRAND FINAL CHORUS OF ENRAGED RIVALS.

Tutti Frutti. *Howlissimo.*

With pitchforks, guns and expletives,
The villain we'll pursue,
And if we catch him, surely will
A massacre ensue.

'Twas ever thus: the favorites
Can never get a place,
In every caucus and campaign
The Dark Horse wins the race.

CONVERSATIONS.

[From the German.]

FIRST COUPLE.

SHE. "Yes, the floor is perfectly splendid, and don't you think that the favors and the flowers are lovely?"

He. "Yes, but (gallantly) I don't think that the flowers are *all* that is beautiful here to-night."

She. "O, really! you quite overwhelm me. Now I suppose I must return the compliment and say that the floor is not the *only* polished thing in the room."

SECOND COUPLE.

He. "Yes, I like it very much, but I can't say that I am a very good player."

She. "O, I'm perfectly fascinated with it. It's such fun to beat, and then you know it's quite the thing to walk around in your tennis dress with your racket. O, here comes that horrid Mr. ——, with a lovely favor. Please excuse me."

THIRD COUPLE.

She. "O, yes, I like Howell's stories very much, but James is so sort of æsthetic, don't you know? And then his young men are so nice. I do think that James' young men are just lovely. By the way, have you seen 'The Portrait of a Lady' in the *Atlantic Monthly?*"

He. "N-no; I have not. Who is the artist?"

FOURTH COUPLE.

She. "Yes, it is very warm."

He. —— —— ——

She. —— —— ——

He. "Isn't it strange how much rain we have had lately?"

FIFTH COUPLE.

She. "O, Mr. ——, I was so sorry not to be able to see you act at the entertainment the other night. I heard that you did splendidly."

He. "Thank you. You are very kind, but my part was an easy one. You see it was a ridiculous sort of thing, and all that was necessary was that one should make a perfect fool of himself."

She (absently). "Oh! Then I should think you must have done it nicely."

SIXTH COUPLE.

He. "Are you a believer in elective affinities?"

She. "Well, really, I have not read much about these scientific inventions lately. This is Edison's latest, I suppose."

SEVENTH COUPLE.

She. "There you go again. I declare, I never saw anything like you young men, talking about getting 'knock downs' to young ladies, and 'great heads' and 'steen cents.' Why, I think it's dreadful. Now what *do* you mean by K. O.?"

He. "Why, 'catch on,' of course."

She. "O, but you know you shouldn't spell it with a *k;* you should spell it with a *c.*"

EIGHTH COUPLE.

She. "But there is one thing that I positively hate, and that is, to be talking to a young gentleman while he is looking all around the room, and have him just turn to me once in a while with a most society sort of a smile, and say, 'Yes,' or something of that sort."

He (who has been gazing intensely at the beautiful Miss S.) "I—I beg your pardon! O, yes, certainly. So do I!"

O maiden sweet,
    With pretty feet,
        And dainty little shoe,
I see thee not,
But yet I wot,
    Thou cheerest for the blue.

Thy hose is blue,
Thy shirt is, too,—
    A sign that ne'er can fail—
'Tis thus I tell,
Aye, very well,
    That thou dost cheer for Yale.

NINTH COUPLE.

He. "But you see, at these bon-fires, we have to be very careful not to be caught; so we generally tie up the tutors."

She. "What! Tie them up? Bind them, do you mean? Hand and foot?"

He. "Ye-yes. O, yes, of course."

She. "Why, I think that's too mean for anything. But do tell me! Do they do any hazing in college now?"

He. "O, yes. They did a good deal in the first of the year, but they had to be very careful about the tutors. Sometimes they make them 'browse,' as they call it. They tie their hands behind them, and then put a piece of paper on the wall above their heads, and make them jump for it."

She. "What! the tutors? Why, I do think you treat those poor men shamefully. But this is the last waltz. Don't you think it would be nice to dance?"

A VALUABLE REMNANT.

EXPLANATORY CORRESPONDENCE.

Dear Mr. Editor :—

HERE is some MS. which I found in a Freshman recitation room a day or two since. It depicts a phase of life familiar to some of us, and as such I recommend it to the classmates of the poor home-sick boy who wrote it.   Yours respectfully,
F—— G——, '87.

Dear Mr. G—— :

Many thanks for your indirect contribution. So little is known as to the customs and habits of this timid, retiring bird, the freshman, that any treatise throwing the least light upon the subject is of great value not only as a matter of interest but also as a real contribution to science.

Yours,   Ed. COURANT.

(The MS.)

Father thinks I'd better go to College. Of course I have great regard for father's wishes, but I don't want to go, all the same. However, as the entire family seem bent on making a student of me, it seems quite probable that I shall be obliged to find quarters away from home this fall. Last evening we had a discussion on the subject. Father took the initiative as usual. "John," says he, "I've been thinking it all over, and I've come to the conclusion that Yale is the place for you." "Very well, papa," I replied,— I call him "papa" in the privacy of our domestic life— "you understand my feelings on the subject and know how averse I am to going, though I must say my own preferences lie with Yale." At this the Governor brightened up with a considerable degree of pleasure and launched out with a good deal of enthusiasm :— "Oh, yes, by all means. They are much more practical at Yale, and they treat the boys in a decidedly more manly way. Then, too, they've abolished all this confounded hazing there, and I'm told that the students have such respect for their instructors that a decree of the Faculty is held as sacredly inviolable as one of the Ten Commandments." The Governor was so manifestly good-natured that I thought if would be quite the proper time to speak of money matters. "Papa,"

THE DEGENERATION OF THE SASH CRAZE.

JUNE, 1889.

SEPTEMBER, 1889.

D   ainty little maiden,
        Tripping forth each day,
        Bearing weighty volumes,
        On your learnéd way.
                This is from the one that passes,
                Going to his daily classes ;
                He that looks with longing eye,
                As you lightly pass him by.

    Dainty little maiden,
    With the nut-brown curls,
    Would that I professor were,
    In your school of girls !
                Passion-plants I'd botanize ;
                Lecture on the *heart*, with sighs ;
                Or, in just a class of two,
                Love's sweet *Art* I'd teach to you.

A VALUABLE REMNANT.

said I, "how much do you propose to give me as an annual allowance, anyway?" "*Five hundred dollars*" was the prompt reply. This exceeded my wildest hopes, for mother had assured me only the day before that three hundred dollars would have to carry me through freshman year, provided I was fortunate enough to get a scholarship, which I think I shall have no difficulty in doing. The subject was dropped at this point, and I went to bed to dream of valedictories and the like.

*   *   *   *   *

It seems an age since I wrote last in my diary. What changes have taken place since then ! I am a student at Yale ! Father (I think I shall call him "*father*" hereafter, as Jo. Blood gave me unlimited game when he heard me speak of "*papa*"), as I was saying, father accompanied me to the train and gave me his blessing and one hundred dollars of my allowance. With all due respect to him, I must say that the latter was the more acceptable. We went to Chapel last Sunday, and it *did* seem refreshing to be addressed as "men and brethren" by our revered pastor. It makes one feel so much more at ease with himself. I glanced over at Jo. Blood, and he was looking as dignified as the minister himself. Jo, by the way, is an awfully good fellow. He gives one unlimited chaff, and rather drives a joke or a pun to distraction by repetition, but he's awfully "tone," don't you know ? "Gad," said Jo. to me, the other morning after chapel, "it's deuced clevah, don't you know, this bowing, ah, to

Prex. Enjoy it 'mensely, 's suah you." I think father must have been mistaken when he said that hazing had been abolished, because Jo told me that the Sophomores made him go through all sorts of performances the other night. Seems funny that they should tackle such a fellow as Jo, though. I thought they always left such swells as Jo alone. They call him "Cheeky" Blood, too. It's awfully rank in them.

*   *   *   *   *

A gentlemanly fellow came around this afternoon and introduced himself as a collector for the Yale Navy. Jo gave him twenty-five dollars, so I put my name down for that amount. He seemed very grateful for it, and said he would send some of his friends up to see me. It was devilish kind of him to take such an interest in me, but I suppose Yale men all take a brotherly interest in each other.

*   *   *   *   *

This diary is getting to be a deuced bore. So is Greek. Father writes me that he expects me to take a very high stand in my class, and I shall endeavor——

*   *   *   *   *

Was interrupted by hazers. As I was remarking, I shall endeavor to——

*   *   *   *   *

Had to stop a moment and answer a man who wants my subscription to the *News*. To proceed, I shall endeavor——

*   *   *   *   *

A *Record* man just broke in upon me. I subscribed. Once more, I shall endeav——

*   *   *   *   *

UNKNOWN.

Sweetest, blithest, fairest,
  Maid of maids the rarest,
Scant my wealth, yet all I'd give to greet thee.
  Long I've waited hoping, hoping,
  But I'm fated, moping, moping,
Ne'er to meet thee.

Walking, gliding, dancing,
  All my heart entrancing.
Ah, the gulf whose boundless depth divides us,
  Smiling softly, smiling kindly,
  Love darts, sped, alas, how blindly,
Thus harsh fate divides us.

No. I haven't any old clothes. Confound these interruptions! I shall endeavor to com——

* * * * *

Gospel Union *News?* Full of interesting matter, for twenty-five cents a year, did he say? I *had* to subscribe. Now, finally, I shall endeavor——

* * * * *

An African who wanted me to buy a brick in the Hallelujah Bethel Church, located in the interior of the Sandwich Islands! To resume my diary, I shall ende——

* * * * *

Said his name was Jim Saunders, and promised to give me a pine-apple when his cargo arrived. I shall endeavor——

* * * * *

Three dollars more gone for the *Lit.* Hang it, I shall end——

* * * * *

[Just here, it is supposed that the class-bore entered, for he *did* "end "——and science is left to grope helplessly on and speculate as to what he intended to say in that last sentence. *"Requiescat in pace."*]

GEORGE WASHINGTON.

[A model Junior Ex. piece, warranted to take the Prize if it gets a chance.]

THE first in war, the first in peace, the first in the hearts of his countrymen, he was born of rich yet honest parents in Virginia. 'At an early age he manifested a predilection for military power by thrashing all the slaves on the plantation. Later he displayed his love of adventure by coon-hunting, and his hardihood by marrying the adorable Martha, whom he first loved from a fancied resemblance to that companion of his childhood's days, the hatchet, and who made him a good wife notwithstanding; it is even said that the thought of her angelic attributes helped him to cross the Delaware. At least he crossed it, for have we not seen the picture? He was made general of the alleged army by Congress, which he conducted to a safe place of retreat in a very creditable manner. He was twice made President, and died greatly beloved. His best literary productions were the Declaration of Independence, the Constitution of the United States, and that of Chi Delta Theta. Of all his great deeds, his first and greatest was to have a birthday, which has been preserved even to this day. His virtues were many, almost as many as his headquarters. Proud yet not humble, strong yet not weak, good yet not bad, noble without being base, he endured adversity without giving way to ambition, and prosperity without yielding to its crushing load. Altogether he lacked but one thing; yet that alone would have swamped him had he taken the stump in our day—he could not tell a lie. May he rest in peace!

SANDWICHES.

[Dedicated to the waiter at the New Haven depot.]

THE dew of night was falling fast
As through the railroad train there passed
A darkey bearing, slice on slice.
Refreshments of this strange device,
  " Sandwiches, fresh cut ham sandwiches,
    Cut fresh for every train."

His eye was black; his lips beneath,
Flashed dazzling white his yellow teeth;
And like a two-cent clarion rung
The warbling of that wagging tongue,
  " Sandwiches, fresh cut ham sandwiches,
    Cut fresh for every train."

" Sandwich this way!" an old man said,
Smoothing the hair on his old bald head;
" But stay! is the ham cut thin and wide?"
Yet soft that sylph-like voice replied,
  " Sandwiches, fresh cut ham sandwiches,
    Cut fresh for every train."

" O cheese," the maiden said, "and rest
A ten cent sandwich on my chest!"
An H_2O stood in each eye,
But still he murmured with a sigh,
  " Sandwiches, fresh cut ham sandwiches,
    Cut fresh for every train."

There in the train, as on its way
It sped, a fresh cut sandwich lay,
And from the depot, a long way off,
Came a noise like the whooping cough,
  " Sandwiches, fresh cut ham sandwiches,
    Cut fresh for every train."

FABLES.

THIS is an examination. See how Sad these Boys look! Look at That Boy in the corner. He will Pass. He has Studied hard. He has all his Knowledge at his Finger-ends. See, He puts his knowledge in his Pocket, because the Tutor is looking. Come away, children!

* * * * *

See that man in Brass buttons. He is Not a General. He is a Policeman. What has He got in His hand? It is a Club. Is it Heavy? Say Good Evening to him and he will let You know its weight. The Policeman is a Man of wrath. Children, "Flee from the Wrath to come." Cave canem et the Policeman.

* * * * *

Is not This a Pleasant looking man? What a Sweet Smile he Has! How softly he speaks! He is a Subscription Man, little children. Run away or He will Take your money with a Smile and cut you Dead the next time He sees You. But He doesn't mean Anything. It is only his Way. but it's a Pretty poor Way, little children.

WHY NOT?

AH! QUEL MALHEUR!

When we were young, when love was play,

We lived in most delightful style,

So artlessly from day to day,

And never knew the rogue the while.

But now, ma foi, I see him smile

Exultingly at all I say.

I know too well his every wile,

And Isabel?   Her love's still play.

INFRA DIG.

HELLO, Erastus!
Good morning, Samuel.

Is the lesson hard this morning, Erastus?

I don't know, I haven't looked at it: he won't call me up to-day.

I haven't looked at it, either.   This is a terrible snap, isn't it?

Yes, but there is one thing I got stuck on.

What was that?

Why, I can't make out whether "dahebeyah" means stove or policeman.

It means stove, of course.

Well, the notes cite this passage : They brought her back to the dahebayah.—*Ulysses Grant's war papers and bull fights in Egypt.*

That's all right; I remember the connection.   She fell overboard, and they put her back again at the stove, so that she could get dry.

Yes, but some thought that she jumped over on purpose, and so they brought her back to the policeman for trying to commit suicide.

Ah, that's an exploded theory.

Well, I will leave it to Jeshubal Ripples.

All right, you can ask him.

Mr. Ripples, what does "dahebeyah" mean?

Dahebeyah is an Indian name for a great chief, the man who lords it over everything else.

Well, how does that sentence about bringing her back to the dahebeyah bear that meaning?

The sentence ought to read : We bring her back to thee, Dahebeyah.

Oh, yes; well, I puzzled over that for an hour.

I thought you said you hadn't studied the lesson.

That's all right.   You ought to know by this time what that means.

ROWDYISM, RUFFIANISM, AND RUSTICITY!

STUPENDOUS AND STARTLING STORIES OF STORMING STUDENTS.

FIERCE FIRES! YALE YELLS!! RAGING USHERS!!!

HALF OF YALE COLLEGE IN ASHES.

LOW-LIVED HARD POLITICIANS IN EMBRYO.

A HISSING HOT-BED OF HELLISH HEATHENISM.

[From the New York Moon.]

NEW HAVEN, CONN.—Things are in a sad state here.   The college has lost its prestige, only thirteen men having entered the freshman class, much to the chagrin of the instructors, who are offering large prizes in money to all new-comers.   The number of students has steadily decreased since the Durfee pump was closed, and it has been computed that the college will be reduced to three students, provided the present rate of decrease continues four more years.

All student meetings bear a close resemblance to a caucus of ward politicians.   Take, for instance, the meeting of the senior class last week for the election of class officers.   A howling mob assembled in one of the college rooms.   No chairman could be selected. So some of the strongest athletes in college fought his way to the chair, of which he took possession with the material assistance of his athletic colleagues, armed with clubs, revolvers, etc.   Comparative quiet was gained at length, and the chairman pro force called, i. e., yelled for nominations for class orator (next to a unanimous election in the Co-operative Association, the greatest honor in college.)   Mr. Parson's name

Apropos of the comforts of travel to-day—
Of the absence of dust—the luxurious way
That one sits through a journey, no matter how far,
May I ask if you've been in the Farmington car ?

The tunnel so long and so poky before
Is passed like a flash—is no longer a bore,
And even its darkness and noise cannot mar
The pleasure one gets in the Farmington car.

You want to play cards with the " boys " in the " smoker ?"
You like the excitement of whist or of poker ?
Talk of whist !   Even poker is tamer by far
Than a good game of " hearts " in the Farmington car.

was proposed, but either because of his unpopularity, or through the efforts of the opposing faction in his class, such a kin and confusion arose that finally Mr. Parsons was compelled to withdraw his name. Mr. Cotton was then nominated, and by dint of hard electioneering and bribery was elected.

After order had been restored, the chairman called for nominations for class poet, Mr. Caught-on T. Loose (private of the Woolsey Battalion), Mr. Scientific School Peeps, Mr. Lahnlady (of the Wreck-ed), and Mr. Dear (President of Φ. B. K.), were nominated with considerable difficulty. The drawn knives and menacing attitudes compelled Mr. Dear's resignation. The ballots were then cast, 843 in number (the class numbers 143), and Mr. Loose was declared elected. Mr. Peeps, blushing red, rose and demanded the unanimous election of Mr. Loose. The loud click of Mr. Peep's revolver being heard all over the room, it is needless to say the motion was carried.

After the smoke from the revolvers had somewhat cleared away and the chairman hove in sight, he called for nominations for class statistician. Amid the general howl which then arose, the chairman seemed to distinguish two names, and printing them on the blackboard (Yale men cannot write), he stepped aside. Again the revolvers belched forth their iron hail. After the six-shooters of the gang had been emptied, the chairman stepped forward, and counting the bullet-holes in the blackboard, declared the one who had the most in his name elected. Business being over, these gentlemen (?) proceeded down town, where, procuring combustibles, they set fire to half the town.

(Later Reports.)

· We have since learned that the above reports are fortunately exaggerated. The conflagration was confined wholly to the college yard, and we are happy to state that not more than half the college is burned. The fire-fiends began their work by setting fire to the first of that series of beautiful buildings which enclose the northwest corner of the campus. Barrels of kerosene were poured upon the burning mass, which lit up the fiendish faces of the students delighting in their wantonness. All the Faculty, and the full police force of the city, including one who bore the scars of a similar encounter, were powerless to quell the raging mob. With difficulty they escaped with their lives. Next morning the campus presented a fearful sight. A large portion of it was a heap of smouldering ashes, sending their pale blue smoke toward heaven, as if invoking vengeance on the ruthless destroyers. As your reporter gazed upon the ruined acres, he heard a hoarse roar of applause proceeding from a neighboring lecture room, where the incendiaries of the night before were eagerly drinking in the seductive doctrine of free trade. This explains it all.

PROM. EXAMINATIONS.

NO definite time is set as a *limit*. There will probably be as much time as anyone wishes. Students will please leave hat, cane and overcoat outside. Write on one side of the paper. No questions must be asked the committee. If you don't understand, or if you can't find your partner, pass on to the next.

1. *Character of the New Haven hackmen :* Modesty, generosity, ingeniousness.

2. *Standard of the New Haven House :* It is as high as ever.

3. *Translate into baby French.*
I believe this your dance will the next be.
Is it not that after the one will you the next have ?
Not so, I think ; let me the card see.
Hegenomy of all Atium ! It is that what you say.
That is too bad. But I will you later again see.

4. *Criticise the following :*

Round and round and back and forth,
  Up and down in the mazy dance,
Twisting, twirling, wheeling, wheeling,
  Heart to heart and glance to glance.

Some are rashly dashing, crashing,
  Hit or miss by the merest chance,
Tripping, gliding, slipping, sliding,
  Now retreat and now advance.

Now the modest h—pin patters
  On the floor with a tinkling fall,
Laces torn, flowers forlorn,
  Lights are out and the guests are gone,
The dance is over and that is all.

Parse the italicized words. Explain my theological reference in line 9 and compare King Lear, Act V, Scene 1. Point out similarities between this and the "Cataract of Sodore." Why is this more poetical ? Parallel passages in Horace ; in Catullus.

A PARABLE.

AND it Came to Pass that in Those days Two Students were Disputing Together, and the "Bird " would have persuaded him who was surnamed "Dig," for his Arts were many, even though his Stand was Low—Even unto Suspension. Moreover, while They were Contending, an Insect called a Recitation did Sting the "Bird," and he Thrust It away From him with Ease. But the "Dig " was Troubled in Spirit and with Difficulty drove the Insect away.

And yet again, as they Stood, a Larger and Terrible Insect called a "Semi-Annual " Drew near, so that the "Bird's " knees smote Together and his Strength Forsook him, and First The Insect Flew at the "Dig," but he withstood It, For he *Was* a "Dig." Then it Drew Near Unto the "Bird," and Stung him, So That he Fell to the Ground, and his Spirit took Its Flight, and the Tutors Did Eat of the Fragments Thereof.

THE MARKING SYSTEM EXPOSED!!!

LEAF FROM THE BOOK OF PROF. MARCUS LOW.

	Thursday, May 1.	Friday, May 2.	Saturday, May 3.	Monday, May 5.	Tuesday, May 6.	Wednesday, May 7.	Average Stand.
T. CENTERFIELD,	✕⁴⁶	✕⁴⁸	A				Undiscovered.
J. DEVELTREE,	△¹⁰ ⁊	¶²⁰?	✕²² ●⎮	✕²⁴ ⸲ N.B.	✕²² ⸲	✕²² ⸲	Not Φ. B. K.
D. FLUNCKE,	✕¹⁶	⎮		⎮¹⁸		⎮	— 𝟪
S. HORSEMAN,		" ⁊ "	— ⎮⁶	✕	" ⁊ "	§¹⁹	.62½
C. RUSH,	[	[!	[!!	⁊	⎮	(	3.41⅚
B. SKINNER,	⎮	?¹⁸	⎮		✕	⎮	Microscopic.
A. SMITH,	● 𝟪³⁰§			[	[²²		Has no av.
V. TUFF,	⎮⁴⁶	⎮	⁊		⎮	⎮§	Below av.
G. O. WEST,	⁊³⁰	[	" ⁊ "	§²²	[²⁴	?	2.25
O. YOUNGMAN,	$1.00 ⎮	⁊⁴	[! ⌓	§⁸	§¹²	✕	2.00

REMARKS AND COMMENTS.

CENTREFIELD. ✕⁴⁶ means cut recitation, 46 marks. A, left on third—for Milford.

DEVELTREE. △¹⁰, bonfire, 10 marks. ⁊ recitation mark, 1.50. ¶, caught him plugging up the key hole, 10 marks. ?, good recitation, but have reason to doubt the genuineness. N.B., letter home. Cut four times on bogus sick excuse

D. FLUNCKE. ⎮, recitation mark, 0.00.

HORSEMAN. " ⁊," translation savors of the turf. — ⎮, minus flunk, saw him using a horse in class. Tried to work the Horseman racket on me again. §, recitation mark, 2.75.

RUSH. Mark the perfect man—but not too high. [!!, 6; cold rush, optional, and manifested great interest. ⁊, 1.50; asked a question I couldn't answer. ⎮, shall have to flunk him once or twice. I find his stand is within .03 of my own. (, 3.99; would have had to mark him 4, if he hadn't stopped to breath.

SKINNER. ⎮, moved him to front seat—recited with his book open. ?, exactly the words of the book. ⎮, linen untidy; looks suspicious. ⎮, studying in chapel. Ought to go to sleep as I do.

SMITH. Saw him on the horse car the night of the rush, 20 marks. [, 4—he has a pretty sister in town. [, another rush. I have just found that his uncle is president of Texas University.

TUFF. ⎮⁴⁶, caught his breath from the back seat. I can't give him any more marks, so I flunked him. ⎮, went to sleep in recitation. ⁊, guess he must have been prompted.

YOUNGMAN. $1.00, scratched his name on the seat. Perquisite 75 cents. Mem.—Will take in the circus and the living skeleton. 4 marks for bringing peanuts into recitation. 4 marks for giggling. 4 marks for applauding my mistake.

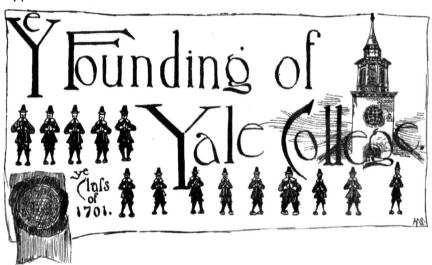

Ye Founding of Yale College. ye Clafs of 1701.

O N a warm May day in 1700, Governor Davenport and Silas Pierpont of New Haven, sat smoking with their
feet upon the railing of their wigwam piazza. " Big frogs in the little puddle " were these men, but no New
Havener ever found it necessary to remind them of that point. They knew it and looked it.

As for the Governor, he was a dark blue Puritan, and ruled New Haven with a rod of iron; what he said
generally "went." But Silas, or Ponty as his friends familiarly styled him, was hardly a second fiddler. He held the entire stock of the Derby road soap factory, owned large tracts of East and West Rocks, to say nothing of an acre or two in the Quinnipiac swamps, and as a pal of the guv'nor's, had free *entree* to the "bung tung" of New Haven society.

'Twas the Governor who at length broke the silence, by asking Silas for a fresh cheroot, which was reluctantly furnished. " I'll tell ycu what, Ponty," said his companion, fingering

SILAS PIERPONT AND GOVERNOR DAVENPORT.

THE GOVERNOR AND SILAS HOLD A MEETING AT BRANFORD.

upon the table. "Look-a-here young man, ain't I in this, too?" angrily interrupted the Governor, with a current expletive, "I founds this college, with these here books," and the enraged magnate slammed down a complete set of Bohn's translations.

How closely we cling to tradition. In all these years that simple act has not been forgotten. We still go to Branford with our Bohn's volumes to commemorate that sacred and solemn rite per-

his diamond shirt stud meditatively, "How would you like to found a college with me?"

Ponty vouchsafed no reply, but reaching carelessly for his flint-lock, blazed away at an object that was squirming along in the grass. The object bounded into the air, and with a wild yelp of Indian profanity, fell dead. "You were saying——?" said Ponty, replacing his musket with cool nonchalance. "To be sure, found a college, well, old man, I'll go you."

The next week, the Governor and Silas held a meeting at Branford, a flourishing swamp a few miles away, with Silas in the chair. "I hereby found a college," said Silas, impressively placing an imported beer stein

THE OBJECT, WITH A WILD YELP OF INDIAN PROFANITY, FELL DEAD.

formed by our forefathers.

Such were the auspices under which our tree of knowledge was planted.

* * * *

Saybrook, a gay art center a few miles away, boasted the advantages of a central location, a steam laundry, and a soda fountain.

Freshmen couldn't be trusted far away from home in those days, and to avoid the threatened *boycot* the worthy founders were compelled to humor the populace, and accordingly shipped the college to Saybrook. But the splendor and renown of the days of a Thanksgiving foot-ball game were yet a long way off. So Ponty and the Governor thought, for, to use Ponty's disgusted expression, " the durned college would

A "QUIET GAME" WITH THE INDIANS.

not draw as well as a fake lottery ticket." The freshmen, too, such as they were, were a bad lot. Totally lacking the subduing influence of sophomore discipline, they were tough and fresh. They rebelled against 5 A. M. chapel, against the bear's meat diet of Saybrook boarding houses, and as the ground floors of the new wigwam dormitories were damp and unhealthy, Ponty, the Governor, and the faculty decided to pull up stakes and sour on Saybrook. Saybrook people objected, particularly the creditors. Tick was a recognized and respected custom in the trade of those good old Puritan times, but a "quiet game" with the Indians now and then, had made the students very bad pay, and Saybrook tailors were not for losing by such a deal. At this crisis a benefactor loomed up, and General Saltonstal was the man. The General's real name has been lost in the obscurity of the past. "Saltonstal" was an Indian sobriquet meaning "too much money," a justly applied title, for the General lived in a brown stone mansion, in one of New Haven's most prosperous suburbs. He had a pond in front of his house, which he afterwards rented to the college boys, for their races.

It was the General who persuaded Eli Yale to emigrate, and to chip in with his pile to help the boys to get away from Saybrook. This Eli did, and when finally established at New Haven, in touching gratitude to Eli, they named the college YALE.

A FENCE ORATION.

BY ISAAC BROMLEY, JR., '81.

Gentlemen of the Class of '82:

On behalf of my classmates and the faculty, I congratulate you on having reached the Sophomore fence. It marks a memorable point in your career, for we cease giving you taffy when we give you the fence. All your studies of Freshman year have been simply to prepare you to sit gracefully on the Sophomore fence. Your victory over Harvard gave you an opportunity for practice in the exercise on the fence up yonder, and we have been gratified to observe that you do it well. So well that it has been remarked by the faculty that it seems to be your best hold. On this subject, President Porter, at a recent faculty meeting, said: "What is there more becoming and ornamental to a fence than a Freshman!" And when Professor Thacher answered, "The Cat," the whole faculty came in on the chorus, "It is indeed the cat." But let it be no discouragement to you to be beaten by the cat. That's what the cat is for.

You have doubtless found out by this time that the members of the faculty do not view you with favor. They have been prejudiced against you ever since you entered college. They said you were too pushing, although you did not seem disposed to shove any, and you knew so much that they were half afraid to try to teach you anything. Like the Irishman on horseback, when the horse put his hind foot in the stirrup, they were ready to say, "If you're going to get on I'll get off." And when we proposed giving you the fence they vigorously opposed it. One professor, whom I will not

name, said, "If you give them a lien on the fence they'll soon have a mortgage on the whole college." Another said, "Give 'em an inch and they'll take an ell." "Take ell," cried the President, "they'll raise it!" But we insisted that you should have the fence, and they reluctantly yielded. I may say to you in confidence, gentlemen, that you are nothing to the faculty, but everything to the class of '81. We have tolerated you when they wanted to fire you out. As soon as they began to know you at the beginning of Freshman year, to see that you were not only handsome but good and great, and that you were liable at any moment to rise up and run the college, they said, "This class must either be totally suppressed or greatly thinned out," and the order given was *decimatum damnum*, which being Latin you will understand better next year. Out of tenderness for you we have refrained from obeying the order strictly. We have slain comparatively few of you, though many have gone and got slewed on their own account. Never forget, gentlemen, that you owe your lives to the forbearance of '81, and whenever you meet an '81 man, be quick to show your appreciation, always remembering that for the preservation of a human life one schooner of lager is but a meager and inadequate return. We had intended, gentlemen, before turning the fence over to you to have veneered it in rosewood and mahogany, upholstered it in satin, built canopies over it and set up foot-rests in front. But when we proposed it the faculty scouted the idea. They said, "With such ears, what need of canopies?" As to foot-rests they made no obj ction except that they must be put inside the fence. They said that the college authorities had no right to permit the class of '82 to sit with their feet on the outside and obstruct the whole street. And one of your own instructors suggested the erection of the market rack with meat hooks on which to hang you by your trowsers.

Disgusted with such frivolous conduct we abandoned the scheme. You, however, at your own expense can do what you like with the fence except carry it off. Take the fence, then, gentlemen of '82, with all its honors and responsibilities. Don't whittle it. Don't desert it. Always have somebody on it. Sit on it constantly and look pretty, and try to reflect honor on the class and credit on the college. Be good, as well as pretty. Don't hoot at processions, or chaff the wayfaring man, or try to sing. Finally, don't put your feet on the cushions, and do not decorate the stove. The fence is yours. Rest your brains upon it.

FINIS.

YALE HUMOR.

Humorous Selections from the University Publications.   Sent on
receipt of $1.50.

Address,

S. A. YORK, JR.,

201 Durfee Hall,

Edition Limited.   New Haven, Conn.

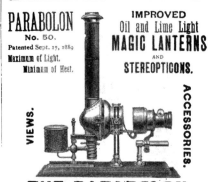

Printed in the USA
CPSIA information can be obtained
at www.ICGtesting.com
LVHW021002101223
766127LV00018B/2100